MAGNIFICENT MARK

DANNY RAY

TABLE OF CONTENTS

ACKNOWLEDGEMENTS

A book is a much more massive project than I ever expected. I have great respect for those who have spoken to me through the written word. There are so many wonderful people to thank for helping me with this book:

To my family for living with me through this process. To my mom and dad for teaching me to be creative, to overcome obstacles, and to be a man of integrity. To my in-laws for your generosity, love, and keeping me focused. To my brother-in-law, Roger Horton for teaching me about the power of storytelling. To my brother and sister, I love you forever. To Joshua Doney for bringing clarity to the book and for the countless hours spent helping me figure out what it really means to leave a Magnificent Mark. To Jon Pilgrim for constantly believing in me—your attention to detail is remarkable. To Lyndsey Brown for shaping and polishing the writing. To Joe Castañeda for your constant encouragement and living an extraordinary life. To the Harris tribe for your ability to press through and never give up.

To my church family—you bring me great joy. To my Bible study group for your constant prayers and support over the years.

There are so many other people I could thank—you know who you are! I appreciate all of you.

Finally, I am so thankful to my God who has shaped my life and redeemed me. Thank You!

*To the brave teens that
choose to live remarkably.*

FOREWORD

I first met Danny Ray at a conference for youth pastors. He performed on stage in front of several thousand participants, and I hung out at his table after the show. He did a card trick with a book of matches that still makes me scratch my head when I think about it.

At the time, I was a youth pastor, and later that year I was putting together an epic back-to-school youth group event for our students. I was scheduling four nights of activities, music and outreach, and it was going to culminate with a mind-blowing experience from a top notch magician.

It's funny to think about now, but I actually called another magician first! That man never returned my calls and that's when a buddy reminded me of Danny's show at the conference we had attended together. I called Danny that afternoon and we scheduled him for our show. A few months later he came out for his performance and we struck up an instant friendship.

My life has never been the same.

Not only is Danny one of the best magicians I have ever seen, he is one of the godliest men I have ever met. When you get to know Danny as I have been privileged to know him, you realize that what you see on stage is what you get in "real life," too. He is genuine in his passion for God, he is truly compassionate toward others, and when he has a chance to speak God's Word to students in a show, he speaks with power, humor and conviction.

So when he told me he was writing this book, I couldn't wait to be a part of the project because I've seen the heart that motivates this guy. God used Danny to challenge me to live way outside of my comfort zone and I know if you'll listen to his heart shared on the following pages -- you will be challenged, too.

I'm fairly confident that what you are holding in your hand is a book that has God's blessing written on every page. As Danny writes about leaving a Magnificent Mark, trust him, because he is living what he writes. And if you follow his godly advice, you'll be leaving a mark of your own in this world, too.

Go ahead, read the book and may your life never be the same!

Joe Castaneda
Founder, Overboard Ministries
www.overboardministries.com

UNLOCKING YOUR AWESOMENESS

YOU ARE NOT A MISTAKE

CHAPTER 1

YOU MAKE MISTAKES, BUT YOU ARE NOT A MISTAKE

Before a first date, it's always a bad idea when a friend says, "I dare you to . . ." Trust me. Anything that follows that statement can't be good, but that is exactly the moment I found myself in. My friend Travis said, "On your date, I dare you to give her a blow nose." Now for those not familiar with a "blow nose," let me explain: you place your mouth over someone else's nose and then blow as hard as you can. If done properly, you can get the person to involuntarily make a honking noise that sounds something like a pigeon being squeezed by a five-year-old. Of course not having much of a social filter at 19 years of age, I said, "You know I will."

So there we were, my future wife and I, out on our first date. We went on a hike to Forest Falls in Southern California to enjoy a waterfall, a picnic, and some great laughs. Then, at just the right moment, I leaned in. She thought I was leaning in for a kiss, but I placed my mouth over her nose and… "HOOOOOOONK!!!" She was in complete shock. Then she let me know that if I ever did that again the relationship would be over! Despite that bad first-date decision, she agreed to a second date, and thankfully, she is still with me 22 years later!

I hope that the insights in this book will help you to avoid making some dumb decisions, will empower you to unlock the awesome person God designed you to be, and will encourage you to make your teenage years truly remarkable.

The reality is that the teenage years will be full of mistakes—it's what you do with those mistakes that matters. You can choose to grow from them or you can choose to let those mistakes shape your life. Mistakes aren't meant to define you. Mistakes may deter you. They may get you off track, but only God gets to define you. Our job is to focus our thoughts and our minds on God's plan for our lives. We are not to look to the left or the right. We look toward Jesus and He will guide us every day.

This will never happen if you believe that when you've made a mistake, you are a mistake. You are not. You are valued by God, loved by Him, and cherished. He just can't get enough of you. His love for you is relentless, it's unending, and it's not contingent on what you do – He just loves you. It's like how you feel when your puppy pees in the house. You don't stop loving it. You love it even though it just made a mess. God is madly in love with you even in your mess. He longs to be in a deeper relationship with you. His heart is always for you, never against you.

UNCERTAIN TIMES

The teenage years are full of interesting twists and turns. Surprise—hair in new places! The pressure of trying to fit in. The unending school work. The complexities of family dynamics. And for some teenagers, unexpected breakups.

12

Tragic death. Divorce. Parents deployed to war zones. Panic attacks. Sexual abuse. Depression. Every day we seem to give our all to God with no guarantees of what pleasures or pains await us. Storms are part of life. They are a way for God to shape us, and it's a way for Him to see what we are made of. The question is, "Will we be able to make it through the storms of life?" The answer is, "Through prayer, yes!"

In Ephesians 3:16, Paul writes, "I pray that out of His glorious riches He may strengthen you with power through His Spirit in your inner being." Paul is not praying this prayer on some island while lying on a hammock in the shade—he is in prison. He has been beaten and is suffering greatly. Prayer that draws you to your knees is a lifestyle, not a momentary awakening to a temporary need. Prayer is simply talking to God every chance you get. It's a longing that is driven by eternity meeting you in your daily life. Is prayer your heartbeat? Do you pray more than just over dinner? More than just for tests? Prayer unlocks your awesomeness. It's only as prayer becomes a way of life that you experience the true power of God transforming you from the inside out.

We never pray to a God whose arm is too short to reach us. No. Our Rescuer is able to do more than we could ever imagine. He has an abundance of grace, love, and awesomeness that He freely gives to us. So, out of His riches, we can pray specifically for strength. Praying for God to strengthen us reminds us that we are not able to gain strength on our own. It reminds us that we are weak and in need of God's power. For some of us, we feel so strong and we have a hard time admitting weakness. It's only when we realize how weak we are, apart from Christ, that He will be able to strengthen us. He doesn't say you can do just a little, or maybe something, but He says you can do zilch, nada—nothing without Him! God wants to strengthen you, so pray for His awesome power to be released in your life.

13

God, in His infinite wisdom, decided that the best way for us to be strengthened would be for Him to make His home within us. God has made His home inside of you. If you believe in Jesus according to the Scriptures, have repented and asked Him to forgive you, then He has made His home in your heart. Your heart houses the eternal God. This should rock your world. By His power we are given everything we need to live each day to the fullest.

HIDING BEHIND A MASK

The sad reality for many Christian teenagers is that they are in hiding. The pressures of trying to fit in—trying to be somebody, trying to make it through school, trying to fake it, push many teens into hiding. Living two different lives, however, causes constant uneasiness. Trying to be one person at school, another at home, another at church, another online—it's overwhelming! Trying to be something you're not born to be never works. It's in hiding that we lose who we are and miss the God who never stops loving us in all of our messiness.

This is exactly what happened with Adam and Eve. The moment they realized they were naked, they went into hiding. God came into the garden to look for them, but they hid. Many teenagers are still hiding, but God is calling us out of hiding and into His light. He is calling us to be transparent. He is calling us to be vulnerable. He is calling us to be risk takers and earth shakers. Your secrets will destroy you. Your secret life will catch up with you and your private life will eventually become public for all to see. How long are you going to hide?

Maybe on the outside you fake confidence, you fake strength, you fake beauty, you fake having a good time, but

14

on the inside you are broken, you are abused, you are hurt, you are bleeding, and you are hiding. Every Christian must take a journey out of hiding and into the open.

Your life might be marked by divorce, marked by loss, marked by depression, or marked by self-injury. But God wants to mark your life with His promises, His freedom, and His wisdom. My early years were defined by abandonment, divorce, and pain. My biological father took off when I was about four years old. Twenty-seven years passed before I saw him again. His abandonment defined my early life. I would wake up with dreams that we would reunite or that he really missed me and really wanted to be my dad. But year after year and day after day, he never came home. I would ask my mom where he was, but she would just say something like, "Probably in jail or off with some woman somewhere." I had an incredible stepfather that loved and cared for me and, with time, became my dad. Yet there was still this longing to be reconnected with my biological father.

I was eighteen years old when I finally found out the truth about my father. Following another dream about reuniting with my "bio-dad," I went to talk to my mom, expecting one of her usual answers. Instead, she led me, along with my brother and my sister, into the living room. She explained that since we were now all adults, we could deal with the information she was about to share. She hesitated

> GOD WANTS TO MARK YOUR LIFE WITH HIS PROMISES, HIS FREEDOM, AND HIS WISDOM.

the way all good parents do, then took a deep breath and went on to explain that Phil, my "bio-dad," was in prison for having sex with a fourteen-year-old girl. My heart was broken. My dream was crushed. As tears ran down my face, my mom explained that she had his address at San Luis Obispo State Prison if any of us wanted to contact him.

At that surreal moment, time stood still. Even though there were a ton of conflicting emotions, I knew I had to contact him. You see, one year prior to that moment, my life had forever changed. It had been 365 days, 2 hours, 18 minutes, and 15... 16... 17 seconds before my mother divulged this information, that I had made a decision to follow Jesus. Not just a decision to go to church. Not just a decision to show up on Sunday. Not just a decision to say one thing, but live another way—No. It was at the age of seventeen that I started living and breathing for my Creator. I knew His love for me was so great that He was crucified for me. I knew that He radically changed my life and I wanted to share what Jesus had done in my life with my biological father, Phil.

With Paul's prison prayer of Ephesians 3:16 echoing through my brain, I wrote Phil and told him that I had a lot of pain, a lot of heartache, but by God's grace working in me, I wanted to tell him, "I forgive you." I went on to tell Phil that God loved him, too, and wanted to be in a relationship with him. It was a painful letter to write, in part because there was a piece of me that didn't want to forgive him even though I knew that's what God was calling me to do. So, I did. I forgave the one who, without saying a single word, hurt me the most in life.

As I look back on that time, I see that God was teaching me to be like Himself. I had to learn to forgive the same way that God had forgiven me. I had to learn to show grace the same way He had shown me grace. I had to learn that it's not enough to treat people the way I think they deserve to be treated, but that I must treat them the way God treats me—with love, with compassion, and with grace. Although Phil and I corresponded a few more times while he was in prison, it would be another thirteen years before we would meet face to face. More on that later. For now, I want you to think about who you need to forgive. Who has harmed

16

you so deeply and caused you so much pain? When will you forgive them?

Some of you might think that the things that have been done to you, or that you have done to others, define you. But remember that your past, your sin, your hatred, and your old life do not get to define you. You are a new creation, daily being made into a wonderful masterpiece. Picture it this way: imagine for a moment that you are in an empty room the size of a basketball gym with four toweringly large white walls. In the center of the room there is a giant prism and to the right of that there is a light that is shining through it. On the wall to your left, there is a beautiful rainbow created by the light hitting the prism at the perfect angle. Now imagine for a moment that I was to take that prism and throw it on the ground. As it hits the ground, it splinters like the screen of a smart phone on a bad day. Next, I pick it up and throw it on the ground again. It continues to shatter. I do this again, but this time it shatters into thousands of pieces over the entire gym floor. Now I pick up all of those pieces and carefully glue them back together. The shattered prism is now permanently marked by cracks and brokenness.

Once that same prism is put back into place and the light shines through it again, for every one of those thousands of cracks, there will be thousands of rainbows shining all over the gym. This is a picture of how God can make something beautiful out of our broken lives. Our lives are broken, cracked, and marked by sin, pain, and struggle. Like the prism, we are fractured, but these marks of our past do not define us. Our mistakes do not define us. Our failures do not define us. Only our Creator gets to define who we truly are and only God knows who He designed you to be. So let His light shine through your fragmented life and create something beautiful out of your brokenness.

ACTION PLAN

Set aside 20 minutes or so to go for a walk. During your walk think about what things are holding you back from becoming the person God wants you to be. Listen for God's voice through His creation.

What masks are you hiding behind?

What would it take for you to come out of hiding and be the person God designed you to be?

What are the biggest pressures you are facing? Ask God to show you His plan for your life.

Our lives are broken and fragmented like that prism. In what ways do you need to allow God to come in and restore you?

Plan another walk with God. Put it on your calendar. Write it on your hand. Do what you have to do to remember to spend time with your Creator.

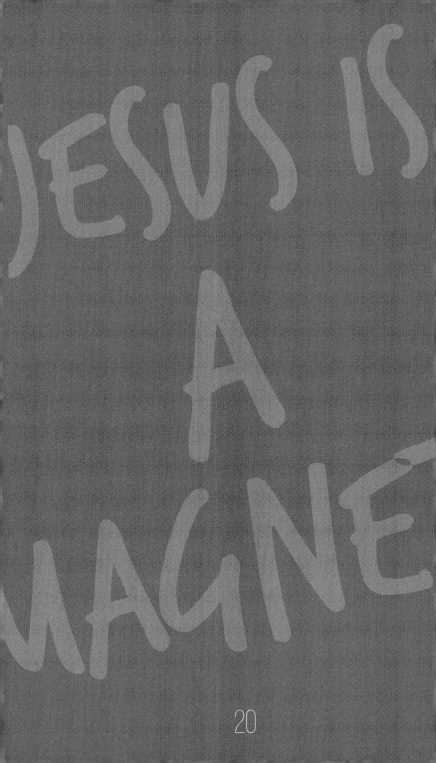

JESUS IS A MAGNE

CHAPTER 2

JESUS IS A MAGNET FOR MESSY TEENAGERS

Jesus loves messy teenagers. The New Testament is filled with stories of Jesus hanging out with hookers, thieves, the mentally unstable, and lots of misfits. Jesus was a magnet for messy people. His heart beats for the broken and lost people of this world. To understand this we need to step back from our phones, from our school, from our city, from our country, and from our world and see things from God's perspective.

A few years ago, my wife and I were enjoying a beautiful spring morning. The cool breeze on a southern California afternoon drifted through our quaint home. Our daughter, Caroline (5), was quietly playing at the computer in our makeshift, Pinterest-designed, re-purposed closet. As my wife Kim and I were talking, Caroline nonchalantly got up, shut both windows and sat back down at the computer. We thought it was a little strange, but continued our conversation until Caroline got up from the computer, approached us, and said, "The game isn't working. It said to shut all the windows, but it's still not working!"

It was a cute, innocent moment where we were able to explain the difference between windows on a computer and windows in a house, but from Caroline's perspective her actions had made sense. She was convinced that she had done everything right and that the machine just wasn't working. Soon, I wondered how many times things seem to make sense from our perspective, when God just smiles at our innocence and patiently takes us on a wonderful walk teaching us to view life through His eyes.

Our perspective can seem right, but it lacks heaven's perspective. Consider this, for example.

• Light travels at 186,000 miles per second.
• In one second, light can travel around the earth seven times.
• 1 Light Year = 5,880,000,000,000 miles, or 5.88 trillion miles.

God can view things over a billion light years away! He can view things from beginning to end. Think about that for a moment. His perspective is wider than the universe, deeper than the oceans, yet God wants to reveal His eternal thoughts to messy teenagers. He is not only able to see every possible angle of every detail of your life, but He is able to see things from the beginning of time to the end of time and, therefore, He sees your exact place in His story. No matter how broken and meaningless your life might seem, you

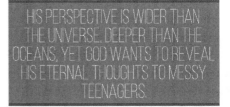

HIS PERSPECTIVE IS WIDER THAN THE UNIVERSE, DEEPER THAN THE OCEANS, YET GOD WANTS TO REVEAL HIS ETERNAL THOUGHTS TO MESSY TEENAGERS.

are designed for a unique purpose. God has crafted your life to create impact and to leave a mark in this world. This is why it's so painful when I hear teenagers describe themselves as "stupid" or "worthless."

Ephesians 2:10 tells us exactly who we are and what our purpose is in this life: "For we are God's masterpiece." That is who you are! And you were "created in Christ Jesus to do good works, which God prepared in advance for us to do." God is not done with you yet! You are His. You are His masterpiece. Let Him finish the good work He began in you and then let Him whisper in your ear His plans to give you hope, to give you joy, to give you purpose, and to give you good works to do for Him.

I have had the privilege of staring into the eyes of the Mona Lisa in Paris, France. After 500 years, she still attracts 1,500 visitors an hour. Why? Because she is a masterpiece. In the same way, you are God's masterpiece, and the Artist is daily shaping you into the remarkable teenager He designed you to be. As we follow God and learn of Him, we too will reflect the craftsmanship of the Master Artist.

GOD WILL CROSS ANY UNIVERSE TO BE WITH YOU

It had been a full day of ministry. The disciples were in a boat crossing a placid lake while Jesus had been taking a nap back in the stern of the rickety vessel. Soon a storm came out of nowhere and huge waves started crashing over the rails of the boat. The disciples, like most of us would, began to panic and quickly became upset with Jesus because He was not helping. He was dreaming about life and rainbows and unicorns, while the disciples were swallowing mouthfuls of water in the bone-crushing storm. Finally, they woke Jesus and desperately asked, "Teacher, don't you care if

23

we drown?" It's funny how easily the disciples forgot who they were with and the power and authority He possessed. Jesus simply said to the waves, "Quiet! Be still!" Then everything in their world became eerily calm.

Silence. Quietness. Speechlessness.
No clamoring. No racket. No commotion.

It's as if the disciples realized, "Umm, Jesus. We forgot that you are in complete control. We forgot that you are the Creator of the heavens and the earth. We forgot that you have all authority over creation. Sorry, Jesus. We are the ones who are small. You are not. Sorry, Jesus. It's just that we forget sometimes that you are the Mighty One."

It was about midnight when the disciples finally docked their boat right next to a graveyard. I don't know if you've ever been in a cemetery in the middle of the night, but it must have been creepy, especially when a naked, bloody, and crazy guy was coming their way. This demon-possessed man could not be chained, and no one was strong enough to overtake him. His problems were so deep, his pain so overwhelming, that he would cut himself with stones. Sound familiar? The idea of cutting is not new by any means. But when this bloody, demon-possessed man saw Jesus, he ran up to Him and fell down on his knees. The demons inside this man begged Jesus not to torture them. So Jesus asked, "What is your name?" The demons replied, "Legion." To give you an idea of this guy's immense struggle, a "legion" was a unit in the Roman army consisting of 3,000 to 6,000 men. So this man was full of an army of demons.

We all face "demons" at different times. This man dealt with a lot of demons, day and night. Jesus confronted this man's demons and commanded them to go into a herd of pigs. So the demons fled into 2,000 pigs and then the pigs jumped off of a cliff. This was a day when pigs actually flew. They were suicidal pigs. Soon an angry mob, outraged that their pigs were flying off of a cliff, showed up in force. You see, the pigs were their only means of clothing and feeding their families and they just could not believe that Jesus had ruined their economy.

When the people came out to survey the damage done, they saw the once demon-possessed man now clothed and miraculously in his right mind. Sadly, the people of the town were only concerned with the loss of their livestock so they begged Jesus to leave.

Jesus crossed an entire lake to heal one crazy, naked, bloody guy. In the same way, Jesus will cross any lake, any ocean, any universe to heal you. Jesus will go to any length to heal one person. I wonder if that person is you? Would you surrender to Jesus? Would you have the strength to tell Jesus how broken and messy you are? To let Jesus come in and clean you up? Jesus longs to cleanse you. He longs to make you whole. Will you let him scrub, wash, and dust you off? Will you let Him in today?

YOUR FOCUS CHANGES EVERYTHING

Shifting our perspective from ourselves to God's plan, His purpose and His Kingdom changes everything. It's easy for us to magnify the struggles in our lives, rather than the love of God and His desire to walk with us through our struggles. Your focus changes everything. If you were to take out a quarter and hold it up toward the sun, you could block out the entire sun. The closer you hold the quarter to your eyes, the bigger it appears. Even though the quarter is infinitely smaller than the sun, it can appear really big. What you focus on doesn't change reality, but it does change your experience with the world around you. Your focus has the ability to make small things appear really big. Here is the beautiful thing about God: focusing on Him reminds us of how small everything is in comparison to Him. This is why David was able to slay Goliath. David wasn't focused on a giant. He was focused on God, and when you focus on God, everything seems small in comparison.

But if you focus on defeat or anger or pain, just like the quarter before the sun, those things will seem so big that they will overwhelm you. You will begin to slip into your old patterns. You will see failure define you, and you will believe that the mess you are in is where you will always be. Instead, focus on the victories you have

DAVID WASN'T FOCUSED ON A GIANT. HE FOCUSED ON GOD, AND WHEN YOU FOCUS ON GOD, EVERYTHING SEEMS SMALL IN COMPARISON.

in Christ. Focus on God even in the midst of pain and He will remind you that He is able to heal, that He is able to restore, and that He is able to make you new.

Since I was a boy, I have studied the art of magic, sleight of hand, illusions, card tricks, and the like. One of the first concepts I learned about was the art of misdirection. "Fake right. Go left." Performing magic would be pointless without misdirection. I have to be able to control where the audience places their focus. I am constantly developing this skill, but I have easily put in 10,000 upon 10,000 hours into mastering misdirection. One of the most fascinating aspects of magic is that people focus on what you focus on. If you want to test this idea, stand in a park and just look up into the sky with your mouth wide open. People will stop and look up into the sky too.

People look where others are looking. Here's the point—if you put your focus on Jesus and not on your mess, then your friends and family (even your enemies) will begin to look in His direction as well. When you focus on Jesus with your words and actions, He will then be magnified in your life. His hugeness will not change, but your perspective will forever change because you are learning to focus on the One who can change your outcome.

CLEAR COMMUNICATION

It can be very frustrating when you are trying to deliver a message and the person who is meant to receive that message just doesn't get it. If I asked you to get me a Mountain Dew out of the refrigerator and you came back with water, somehow we miscommunicated. If you asked a friend to take a picture with you and she started to show you pictures of her family, somehow you miscommunicated.

One time, my middle child, Spencer, was having a hard time receiving a message from his mom. Thankfully, his brother Brian was able to deliver the message. First, let me say that my boys are totally different individuals in the morning. Spencer wakes up at full speed. It's not uncommon for him to run out of his room the moment he wakes up. On the other hand, it takes Brian some time to even realize that he is no longer in bed.

On this particular Monday morning, Spencer was around four years old and Brian was about six. Brian was lying on his mother's lap trying to wake up. As my wife Kim was gently rubbing Brian's back, Spencer appeared and said, "Mom! Today is Friday! Candy Day!"

"No, Spencer. Today is Monday," replied Kim.

But Spencer insisted, "No. It's Friday!"

"No. Today is Monday," stated Kim. "Yesterday was Sunday and tomorrow will be..."

"No, Mommy. It's Candy Day," continued Spencer.

Patiently, Kim tried again to review the days of the

week with him, "No. Yesterday we went to church. Today is Monday. Tomorrow is Tuesday," and so on until, "Then it's Friday! Candy Day!"

"No, Mommy," Spencer repeated, "Today—"

At this point, Brian sat up, smacked Spencer across the face as he declared, "It's Monday," and then laid back down.

All of us were shocked by Brian's actions, but then we all burst out laughing! And after much laughter, Spencer declared to his mother, "I guess it's Monday."

Talk about clear communication—Spencer got the message! Now I am not condoning slapping your family members to get their attention. What I am saying is that you need to wake up and get slapped back into reality to understand that, just as Jesus crossed the lake in the storm to heal the demon-possessed man, Jesus is crossing time and space, land and sea to be with you. He is trying to send you a very clear message. Jesus loves you as you are, even in your mess. In fact, the Bible says "that while we were still sinners, Christ died for us" (Romans 5:8). It's not when we get our lives all together and it's not after we are cleaned up. No. No. No. God's message has always been that He loves us in our mess. He enters into our mess. He stays with us in our mess. And, yes, He cleans up our mess. And when we mess up again and again and again, He keeps cleaning us, loving us, and whispering to us, "I love you no matter how messy you are!" When you forget that, I hope someone slaps you back into reality!

ACTION PLAN

Write down Ephesians 2:10 and tape it to your mirror, computer, or someplace that will remind you daily that you are God's masterpiece.

Like the disciples in the boat, we often forget about God's power. What can you do today to remind you of God's power and plan in your life?

In what ways do you need to surrender to Jesus? Share this with someone.

How can you plan on focusing more on God than on your problems? Place a quarter in your pocket and let it remind you that God can handle all of your problems.

Remind someone today through social media, a text, or face to face that Jesus loves messy teenagers.

FAITH UNLOCKS AWESOMENESS

CHAPTER 3

FAITH UNLOCKS AWESOMENESS

You are loved by the Ultimate Lover. You are chosen by the Creator of the Universe. You are the apple of God's eye. You are your Daddy's child. You are a heavenly gift. You are fearfully and wonderfully crafted by the hands of God. As you discover and believe who you are, it changes everything you say and do.

We need real awesomeness in our lives. We don't need the cheap substitution of awesomeness that is daily offered to us—if we are rich, if we are famous, if we are sexy, if we have a certain number of "likes," then we are awesome. Our world is saturated with this definition of awesome, but don't get infatuated with a poor substitute. God is the awesome One. He is the Creator of awesomeness and our awesomeness begins and ends with God creating us in His image. Our awesomeness is only a reflection of our God. We are made and fashioned by His hands and God alone makes us awesome.

We are not talking about an awesomeness based on our position in this world, but on our position in Christ.

Not based on our sweet ride, or our iPhone 77, but on our abundance of unseen treasures stored for us in heaven. Not a power that is based on your latest selfie, your school, or your social ranking, but a power that raises the dead, heals the sick, speaks universes into existence, and transforms cutthroat,

YOU ARE LOVED BY THE ULTIMATE LOVER. YOU ARE CHOSEN BY THE CREATOR OF THE UNIVERSE. YOU ARE THE APPLE OF GOD'S EYE.

gossiping-haters into peaceful, loving, awesome teenagers. The more you live for Him, and the more your awesomeness will be seen by the world and that awesome-factor will point to how incredible and amazing and awesome God is.

We live in a world where we are constantly trying to achieve. It's about getting the next trophy, the next grade, the next job, the next college, the next girl, or the next party. But achieving leads to a road of regret if we are only doing it to feel better about ourselves. Sadly, some teenagers know this too well. The only time they ever get attention is if they achieve something. They are taught that if you work hard, you achieve. If you work hard, you get approval. If you work hard, you get praise. So when they start to follow Christ, they believe the lie that God loves them based on what they do, not because of who they are. This leads to performing for God to receive His grace. But the Bible teaches us that "it is by grace you have been saved, through faith—and this is not from yourselves, it is the gift of God—not by works, so that no one can boast" (Ephesians 2:8-9). We cannot earn God's love or favor. It is a gift freely given to us that demonstrates His goodness, not our own.

In God's Kingdom, being comes first and doing comes second. It's not that you don't work hard. It's not that you aren't disciplined and it's not that you don't train to be godly. It's that grace is always given first and your actions are to follow out of praise, thankfulness, and joy, not out of seeking approval by what you do and attempting to earn grace. What a curious statement Paul makes in Philippians 3 when he says we need to "live up to what we have already attained." This is kind of like a bank account. If you had money saved up, you could go get what you have already attained—your hard-earned cash. What has God already attained for us? Blessing. Hope. Forgiveness. A future. Redemption. Grace. Purpose. Wisdom. Promise. The list goes on and on. Paul shifts his focus from living according to our plans to living up to what has already been attained for us. Instead of letting the past define who we are, Paul suggests that the new life, not the old life, gets to define us. Once we start living up to the things that have already been attained for us, we will unlock the awesome life God designed for us.

JARS OF OIL

I've always resonated with the concept that "anyone can count the seeds in an apple, but only God can count the number of apples in a seed." There is no way anyone except God can know the potential of any particular seed. God can see which seed will produce thousands of trees, feed millions of people, and live to its full potential. God also sees who we are today and who we could be if we live with Him daily. There is a beautiful story in 2 Kings that unlocks some powerful principles about our potential.

A woman, distraught from the recent loss of her husband and burdened financially because her husband had died in debt, approached Elisha for help. Elisha was a man of God, a prophet, and counselor. She reminded Elisha of her husband's passion and love for God, but feared her children might be taken from her because of the money she owed. She was that broke. She couldn't even take care of her family.

33

In the midst of her suffering Elisha asked her what she had that was of any value. Initially she said, "Nothing." Then, she remembered something that had so little value she hadn't even thought about it: "A small jar of olive oil," she replied. It's as if she said, "I guess I have a small jar of olive oil. I mean, it's tiny. It's hardly worth anything."

Elisha got excited about this little amount because he knew that God could use little things and make them great. He knew that God works out of the barren womb, out of a widow's two mites and how, out of nothing, God created the world. He told her to go knock on doors, go to the market, go talk to every neighbor, and ask them for empty jars. And, listen closely to this next part, he said, "Don't ask for just a few!" Elisha knew God was going to do something amazing, but it was going to be in direct proportion to the widow's faith. So he told her not to get just a few jars. Then he explained the miracle God was about to do. He told her that all of the jars she got would be filled with oil from her one small jar.

The woman's family then went on a mission to collect as many jars as they could. When they went back to her house, each jar was filled one at a time until her sons brought her the last jar; only then did the oil stop flowing. Elisha told her that she could use the oil to pay off all of her debts and live on what was left.

FOUR PRINCIPLES THAT UNLOCK YOUR AWESOMENESS

1. DON'T SUFFER ALONE

Even under great stress and suffering, the widow sought wise counsel. We are not designed to suffer alone. God has designed a community for us in which to share the joys and sorrows of life. It's easy for us to get trapped into a worldly way of thinking that is independent of community. The American way — "pull yourself up by your own bootstraps" — is not only unbiblical, it's a harmful thought process that detaches us from God and each other. It's not until we humble ourselves and call on others that God will reveal different parts of His plan to us. Unlocking our potential requires us to be a part of community.

2. GIVE EVERYTHING YOU HAVE

We might look at our resources and not see any value, but remember that God sees the apples in a seed. Our job is to offer everything we have and everything we are to Him. He sees the potential, not only in what we have, but in who we can become when we give everything to Him. Many people fail to understand the key principle about giving: giving is our greatest resource in changing the world. It could be giving our time, our knowledge, our money, or our resources, but whatever it is we give, giving changes us and the world around us.

In 2008, I decided I wanted to give big. I began to think about my most valuable possessions and how I could give them away. Of all the things I owned at that time, the ones with the most value to me were my magic books, collected over the first 25 years, which I used to study the art of illusion. My wife can attest to the fact that I constantly read those books. I would sift through them and practice new ideas I found in them. At any given time I would have 10 to 15 of those books opened around my office with notebooks full of new ideas. Those books didn't just sit on my shelves. They were tools I used to develop and create new material.

At that point in my life, I was teaching the art of magic to eight students around the country, from Hawaii to New York. I went to the store to buy eight large cardboard boxes and started thinking about each student's expertise. I divided the books among the boxes. Some of the books were over one hundred years old and some were selling for hundreds of dollars on eBay. The week after sending out the books, phone calls and e-mails came in thanking me. I really believe this was the best thing I did in 2008.

Here's the crazy part. The students grew in their ability to create moments of awe and communicate the Gospel. At the same time, I was more creative in the last few years than ever before! Not having the books forced me to think magically, without them, and I'm a better magician for it. The point is that we have opportunities to change ourselves and the world around us by putting this giving principle into practice.

3. MIRACLES REQUIRE FAITH

What would you do if a mentor of yours told you to go knock on the neighbors' doors and collect jars? Would you go to a few houses? Would you go to friends' houses or strangers' houses? Would you go to any houses? It's kind of a strange request. For us to experience the miraculous power of God in our lives, we need to live outside of our comfort zones. Sometimes to experience God's blessings, you are going to have to humbly ask those around you for what you do not have. God's blessing was in direct proportion to the widow's faith. Had she just asked for a few jars, God's blessing would have stopped at a few jars.

What if you really believed that God could fill up the empty jars in your life? What if you constantly brought everything you have to God? You would see God do amazing things with everything you give to Him.

4. GOD LOVES THE WORD "AND"

God loves the word "and." We never know what we are going to get with that word. It could be something great or it could be the most disastrous thing ever, but either way, "and" packs a punch. If you want to see just how powerful "and" can be, check this out. If your youth pastor said, "Hey, we are going out for pizza and . . .and . . . and . . ." your brain would begin to picture all kinds of options. You might have said, "Are we going out for a movie, too? Are we going bowling, too? And what??? Come on, tell us!" If she said, "And a movie with all of your friends" or "And Disneyland!" you might have given her the Youth Pastor of the Year award. However, if she said, "And a car wash!" she would have had some unhappy campers on her hands. The longer she let you dream about what followed that powerful little "and," the better it would have had to be!

For the widow, all of her debt was paid off and her family was able to live on what was left. God's provision came in miraculous proportions. It would have been enough to have her debt paid off, but God loves providing in amazing ways for His children. The word "And" is one of the ways that He surprises us.

Don't go into today with "just a few jars." Approach today with faith in God's power to deliver and to deliver even more, for today is a new day! It's a day that's full of potential. It's a day that can bring you closer to the person that you are designed to be. This is the time to not just talk about faith, but to be faithful. This is the time to embrace the life that God has given you.

DAY AND NIGHT

The day I got dropped off for college and hugged my parents goodbye, tears ran down my face. Not cowboy Eastwood tears, these were pure sobs of homesickness. Nine days later those tears were gone forever. Yes, I met a girl. She was seventeen years old with an amazing story and heart for God. Before her freshman year, she spent three months in Mexico building houses for the poor. I was a follower of Christ at that time, but I am pretty sure I spent the summer playing

37

Donkey Kong or something equally as trivial. Yet this young lady had a passion for Christ that inspired me, and showed me love in action. Everything about her was fascinating to me. I started spending a lot of time with her. We would have breakfast together and sometimes lunch. Before I knew it, we were having all our meals together and probably a few snacks, too. We would talk about family, love, and living for God. I just couldn't get enough of her. Four short years later, I married that wonderful lady.

Our relationship with God is supposed to be like a love relationship. He is supposed to be the One we dwell on, daydream about, and love with everything in us. He is supposed to be the one we run to when times are hard. The One we praise. The One we think about, dream about, and hope for. He is our Savior and Rescuer. The One we are to pursue. Psalm 1 describes it this way: "Blessed is the one...whose delight is in the law of the Lord, and who meditates on his law day and night." Day and night our heart is designed to beat for our God, our King, our Love, and our Life. Do you lose sleep pondering the greatness of God? Are you in love with God? If not, are you missing the point? The person that can't get enough of God ponders His vastness day and night; they think about the depths of His love; they ruminate on His Word constantly.

Life in Christ is meant to be lived to the fullest. Each day, we are designed to wring out all of the love, joy, wonder, wonder and adventure from our lives. Some of these experiences will come through sorrow and pain, and other experiences through laughter and happy times. The

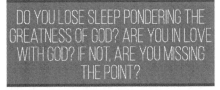

DO YOU LOSE SLEEP PONDERING THE GREATNESS OF GOD? ARE YOU IN LOVE WITH GOD? IF NOT, ARE YOU MISSING THE POINT?

key isn't our circumstances—it's our ability, through Christ, to make the most of every opportunity. We are designed to live for our Lord and Savior. Every day we need to be moved by His grace and His love. Jesus constantly calls us to live life for Him. We have a choice: continue to live in Him or continue to experience life without Him. But life without Him is temporary. It's like diving into an ocean and looking at all the wonders below the ocean's surface. It's beautiful and exhilarating but at some point you have to come up for air. Jesus is our air. You can experience some amazing things without him, but they will come to an end quickly. Yet when you choose to live in Him, you will experience the most amazing life you could ever have.

ACTION PLAN

What are you going to do today to fall in love with your God? Write down one of these verses and meditate on it today:

1. "Jesus knew that the Father had put all things under his power, and that he had come from God and was returning to God." John 13:3

2. "He is before all things and in Him all things hold together." Colossians 1:17

3. "'For my thoughts are not your thoughts, neither are your ways my ways' declares the LORD." Isaiah 55:8

What are some things you own that you value? Give something away to someone to help build God's Kingdom.

EMBRACE YOUR AWKWARDNESS

EMBRACING MYSTERY

CHAPTER 4

EMBRACING MYSTERY

LOCKING PINKIES WITH A GIRL

My heart was racing. My awkward junior high body was sweating. I liked a girl, but I didn't know if she liked me. That day, I was going to find out. I was trying to find an excuse to talk to her before we entered the theater, so that it wouldn't be obvious that I wanted to sit next to her. Two hundred other students from our school were with us on the field trip to see a musical. I wanted to make it look like it just happened to work out that I sat next to her. I found her, made some small talk, and before I knew it we were in the theater sitting next to each other.

But then what? I had heard about these giants of the dating world that would act like they were yawning. They would stretch their arms out, but instead of returning their arms to their side, they would land one arm around the girl. The girl would move closer to the guy and rest her head on his shoulder. The wedding bells would ring and they would live happily ever after. In my eighth grade brain, I knew that if I put my arm around her and she said, "Ew! Gross! Like, what are you doing?!"—it was the 80s and girls talked like that—it would have been awkward. And that would have been too much rejection for me at that time in my life.

As I looked down, I noticed her arm resting on the armrest between us. I thought, "I'll reach out for her hand," but then thought, "What if she says, 'Get your nasty hand off me!' and moves her hand away from mine?" This was still too much rejection and there was nowhere to hide my embarrassed face if that happened. But I had to find out if she liked me. Then I came up with this brilliant idea: I would just go for her pinky! That was about as much rejection as I could handle. If she moved her pinky away from me, I would act like it was just a mistake.

For what seemed like centuries, I looked at her pinky, then back up at her to make sure she was still watching the musical. Then, I would look at her pinky, back at her, and then back to watching the musical. Finally, it was my time to go for it. I lifted my hand and touched her pinky. Her pinky was touching my pinky. Our pinkies were touching! Then it happened… our pinkies locked. It was magical!

I did it. I held her pinky. I was on cloud nine. Life was amazing! Two weeks later, she broke up with me. Welcome to Junior High!

My story, like every teenage story, was the story of the unknown. What happens if? We want to know that if we take a risk, we will be safe. We want to know that God will be there to catch us. We sweat. We fear. We wonder. But at some point we have to make a decision to go into the unknown. There is never a guarantee that our pinkies are going to "lock," but those who never risk anything, never gain anything. Those who never trust God—with their dreams, their hopes, and their fears—never experience God's dream being fulfilled in their life. And His dreams for you are even bigger than your dreams for yourself. He says he wants to give you "immeasurably more than all you can think, ask, or imagine" (Ephesians 3:20). God has huge plans and dreams for your life.

What's ahead of you? Only God knows. He knows the plans He has for you. He knows the purposes He has for you. So the only thing you can do every day is risk locking pinkies with Him. You embrace Jesus' story. His life. His way. God's dream for you will bring you to your full potential. God's dream for you will unravel your gifts, your purpose, and your destiny. His dream for you fits perfectly into His story. His dream for

WHAT'S AHEAD OF YOU? ONLY GOD KNOWS. HE KNOWS THE PLANS HE HAS FOR YOU. HE KNOWS THE PURPOSES HE HAS FOR YOU.

you may require that you risk embarrassment, that you risk your reputation, or that you risk your life—but it's all worth it. You will never regret giving your all to Him.

But we must let Him shape us, move us, and teach us to be like Him. As we do this, we will become the remarkable people God designed us to be. God's dream for us can only be fulfilled when we surrender all of our life to Him. It's not until we give everything we have to Him that we can begin to experience His dream for us. I want to look at the familiar story of Peter walking on the water as a way of embracing the mysteries of God. In this story, we find some extraordinary lessons in a man daring to risk everything to follow Jesus.

GET OUT OF THE BOAT

Have you ever had a really hard day? I mean, a super hard day, like having your best friend get his head cut off!? That would be a rough day, to say the least. That's the kind of day Jesus was having. His cousin John was beheaded and he had just finished feeding 20,000 hungry people. He was exhausted so He sent the disciples away. He climbed a mountain and was finally alone. He spent time talking with His Father and He found peace, rest, and comfort from His Daddy. This is where our story begins.

Jesus was on the wet, sandy waterfront and the disciples were in a boat about three miles off the coast. It was past midnight and it was raining. Nobody was around so Jesus got on the water. Yes—actually on the water.

How long would it take you to run three miles? 20 minutes? 30 minutes? (For some of you, that thought is just killing you right now!) The average person walks at three miles per hour. That means to walk one mile would take about 20 minutes. Now I don't know how long it would take to walk a mile on water, but I can't imagine that it would be less than 20 minutes. That means that Jesus was walking, running, dancing, and/or cruising in the storm for at least an hour before he met the disciples, three miles off the shore. We don't know what that walk looked like, but it must have been an amazing time of Jesus enjoying His own creation. I imagine Jesus was having a blast before His disciples saw what appeared to them to be a ghost.

Around three in the morning, the disciples were doing everything they could to make it through the storm. By that time, the waves were crashing all around them when, in the distance, they saw a shadowy figure on the water. Things were scary enough in the middle of the night. Now they saw someone on the water! They freaked out. Can you imagine what you would do if you saw someone, or something, walking on the water in the middle of the night? That was some scary stuff.

Jesus, seeing their fear, immediately said to them, "Take courage! It is I. Don't be afraid" (Matthew 14:27). Now

Peter got a crazy idea—and I mean crazy! He looked over at the disciples, looked back at the shadowy figure, and said, "Lord, if it's you, tell me to come to you on the water." Keep in mind that Peter did not know for sure whether or not this "ghost" was Jesus. If Jesus wasn't who He claimed to be, Peter was going to sink. Peter was possibly going to die. But Peter recognized the voice. He began to enter into the biggest mystery of his life. He began to trust Jesus in the storm.

Jesus didn't give him a sermon. He didn't tell Peter that He would keep him safe. He simply said, "Come." What are you doing right now? Jesus is standing on the water inviting you to "come" and join Him for the adventure of your life. You can stay in the safety of the boat. You can enjoy the comfort of what you know. Or you can respond to the call of Jesus into the storm, into the unpredictable, and into the wild adventure of following the call. Jesus is calling you to come. What are you going to do?

It might seem safe to stay in your comfortable little boat and do what you have always done, but the safest place is always to be with Jesus. It may seem crazy and it is definitely going to stretch you because it means doing the impossible. News flash: You can't walk on water without

JESUS IS STANDING ON THE WATER INVITING YOU TO "COME" AND JOIN HIM FOR THE ADVENTURE OF YOUR LIFE.

Jesus. But with Jesus you can experience the impossible. This story was not just about walking on water, but about obedience to the call. Jesus calls us into an unpredictable life of suffering mixed with joy, love fused with sorrow, and awkward moments where you embrace your fears. It's a life that experiences fullness because it does not live in the apparent safety of "the boat," but risks everything by stepping out of the boat to be with Jesus.

You can make all the excuses you want.

"I don't have time."
"I don't have the skills."
"I'm too messed up."

Jesus is still calling you! Until you have faith to get out of the boat, you won't experience the power of God in your life. Today, don't just read this story. Take a step of action and get out of the boat!

"Lord, if it's you," Peter replied, "tell me to come to you on the water."

"Come," he said.

Then Peter got down out of the boat. (Matthew 14:28, 29a)

Can you imagine what the other disciples were saying? I am sure they were talking about Peter running his mouth again. I am sure they thought he would sink. I am sure they thought he was crazy. Yet Peter was completely focused on Jesus. He didn't listen to the haters, the boat-sitters, the naysayers—His eyes were locked on Jesus. He wanted to follow Jesus anywhere. He wanted to be like his Teacher, his Master, and his Lord. So Peter risked everything.

Put yourself in Peter's position for a moment. He knew when he stepped out of the boat that he might sink into the abyss. He knew that this could have been his last breath. He put his life, his image, and everything on the line. He was at the edge of the boat with his heart pounding and hands shaking. Then the moment of truth came—Peter got out of the boat and "walked on water and came toward Jesus" (Matthew 14:29b).

Peter did it. He was completely focused on his Savior. Now, we don't know the distance that Peter walked, but we do know Jesus was far enough away that nobody recognized

Him. So Peter had to walk on water for some distance. As he was walking, though, he lost focus. There was a moment when Peter realized that He was in the middle of a storm and outside of a boat! Instead of being captivated by Jesus, he began to notice his distance from the boat, the power of the wind, and the chaos of the waves. So when he lost focus, he began to sink.

Isn't it easy for us to lose focus? We get so excited about doing something great for God, but we check our phone, we text our friend, we hear the latest news, and then we lose focus. We see the storm, the circumstances, and the problems, but fear grips our heart.

But when Peter began to sink, he prayed one of the best prayers in all of the Bible. Not one word could be taken out of his prayer. Peter cried out, "Lord, save me!" (Matthew 14:30) You have to know who can save you: Jesus can. You need to know who needs saving: we all do. No matter what your storm is today, Jesus can save you. Maybe you're fighting addiction. Maybe your heart is broken because you have been used. Maybe the pressure of fitting in is too much. Maybe you just feel unloved and worthless. Listen. Jesus loves you. He is the one who can save you and give you new life—daily. New purpose—daily. New hope—daily.

Jesus can save you, but you have to cry out to Him. As soon as Peter cried out, Jesus "immediately" (Matthew 14:31) reached out His hand and caught him. Jesus can immediately catch you. He is that powerful. His desire is to seek and save the lost, the messy, the broken, and the wandering. He is looking for you to cry out to Him today and say, "Jesus, I can't make it on my own! I need you. I am desperate for you. Come into my life and transform me daily to be like you. Jesus, save me."

Did Peter fail? Possibly. But if Peter failed, he failed on the water with Jesus. I would rather fail a thousand times with Jesus than sit in a boat passively watching God do the impossible. There were eleven other disciples that would never know the grip of Jesus in the middle of the water because they never got out of the boat.

Don't miss an incredible opportunity to see God do the impossible. Get out of the boat. Don't let the storms cause you to stay in the boat. Get out and watch God show up. He showed up in the lion's den. He showed up in the fire with Shadrach, Meshach, and Abednego. He showed up with David, as a teenager, when he beheaded Goliath. He

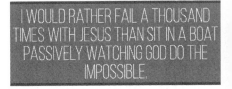

I WOULD RATHER FAIL A THOUSAND TIMES WITH JESUS THAN SIT IN A BOAT PASSIVELY WATCHING GOD DO THE IMPOSSIBLE.

showed up in a manger as a baby. He showed up with Peter on the water. God still shows up in astounding ways and at unexpected times for teenagers that listen to His call to "come."

ACTION PLAN

What can you do today to give your worship to Him?

What do you need to do today to get out of the boat?
Maybe getting out of the boat is:

1. Breaking up with your boyfriend or girlfriend.
2. Turning off the internet in your room.
3. Inviting your friend to church.
4. Going to church.
5. Forgiving your dad or mom.

Write down what you believe God's plan is for you this
week, this month, and this year.

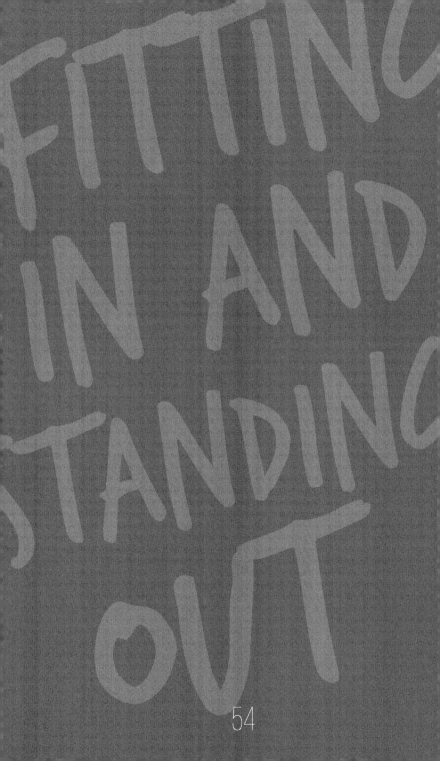

FITTING IN AND STANDING OUT

CHAPTER 5

FITTING IN AND STANDING OUT

Sometimes you don't fit in.

David was a shepherd boy who was overlooked by his entire family before he became a giant-slayer.

Moses was 80 years old when he discovered God's plan for him to deliver God's people out of slavery. He was a wandering fugitive and, at 80, God made him into an outstanding leader.

Mary was a teenage servant of God who definitely stood out. Imagine telling your mom or dad, "Yes, I'm a virgin. Yes, I'm pregnant!" Her worship of God led to the extraordinary life of birthing the Son of God.

Abraham was 100 years old when God gave him a son. Imagine showing up to kindergarten with your 105-year-old daddy!

Sometimes you don't fit in. You stand out. For us to discover who God designed us to be, we have to stop trying to fit in, stay the course, and spend time in His presence daily. But it's difficult to stay on course when so many people are enticing you to a life off God's path.

STAYING THE COURSE

I have had the privilege of partnering with more than 1,000 ministries and churches around the world. Many of these ministries blend into one amazing experience. Yet, there are several people and ministries that stand out for one reason or another. One guy, Paul, is a youth pastor in Montana. He is truly an amazing man of God. He is in charge of three youth ministries. Yes, three! He leads one on Tuesday, one on Wednesday, and one on Thursday. One ministry is in his home town, and the other two are about two hours away from him. Oh, did I mention he has a full-time job as well? He is so passionate for Christ. I love just being in his presence.

The last time I partnered with him in ministry, he let me borrow his car to get to the airport. In Montana, there is no shortage of wildlife and animals along the roads, which can sometimes make driving hazardous. Paul, knowing the potential dangers of the road, left me with this advice: "Danny, I have lived in Montana my whole life. I know many people who have died or been seriously injured taking this road to the airport. If you see a deer, don't dodge it. You hit it and stay the course. There is no room to swerve. Hit it and we will deal with the damages later."

His words about "staying the course" have stuck with me through the years. What would happen if, in every area of my life, I stayed the course? What if instead of trying to fit in, I stood out because I was faithfully living God's plan for my life? What if I didn't swerve to the left or to the right, but I stayed focused on the road ahead of me? When obstacles came, I would go through them and not around them. God's word is clear on the importance of "staying the course." Soak these words into your soul today from the book of Proverbs: "Do not swerve to the right or the left; keep your foot from evil" (Proverbs 4:27).

The easiest way for us to get distracted is by looking to the left or the right and thinking something or someone is better than us, funnier than us, or smarter than us. Instead of focusing on mistakes, problems, and heartache, stay the course and focus on what God has for you. As you do this more and more, you will discover the joy of standing out for the right reasons, instead of fitting in for all the wrong reasons.

LISTENING TO GOD'S VOICE

Recently, I was on the white sandy beaches of Florida for a family trip. The view was absolutely amazing. My sons, Brian and Spencer, and I bought three sketchy boogie boards for seven dollars each and took off for the beach. We were in the water having a blast, not knowing that my wife was calling out (screaming might be a better word) to us from the shore.

We weren't that far away from her, but when you are that close to the crashing waves, it's hard to hear the voice of sanity calling you. My wife, Kim, was calling us for lunch. Apparently, we hadn't eaten in a while. We had lost track of time and had missed the call for us to come in.

Hearing God in the midst of a noisy world is essential for life. If you don't hear His voice, it will be easy for others to steer you off course. Here are three ways we can hear God's voice in the midst of the storm. Like Peter, we:

1. LOOK IN GOD'S DIRECTION

He is always seeking you. He is always with you. God is constantly reminding His wayward children, "I will be with you. I will be with you. I will be with you." In fact, more than any other promise in the Bible, God promises that He will be with us. Why? Because we so easily forget that God is with us. Peter in the midst of the storm kept His eyes on Jesus. Keep your eyes on Jesus.

57

2. MOVE TOWARDS JESUS

Peter moved toward Jesus. The waves are loud, but they aren't louder than God's voice! Yes, God can speak in a whisper, but God can also shout, above any storm in your life, "Come." Keep moving toward Jesus daily. Spend time in the Bible listening to His voice. Spend time in prayer. Spend time talking with other followers of Christ. As you do these things, you will be moving toward Jesus.

3. CRY OUT TO JESUS

Immediately cry out to Jesus when you look to the left or the right and let Him pick you up. You are not perfect. You will make mistakes. You will fail. It's what you do when you fail that will determine the outcome of your life. Will you call out to Jesus and let Him rescue you?

Learning to listen to God's voice changed the course of my life. I was 18 years old and I had the opportunity of a lifetime when I met a world-renowned magician at one of my shows. After my performance, he told me that he would soon be traveling to Caesar's Palace in Las Vegas, then onto New York, and finally on a tour throughout Europe. "I want you to go with me, Danny," he said. "I will train you, show you the ropes, and show you what it takes to be a world-class magician."

I was so excited. This would be a dream come true. There was just one problem. One year earlier I had started a different pursuit. At the age of 17, I made a decision not just to go to church, but to follow Jesus in every area of my life. So I prayed about the opportunity offered by this magician and felt God nudging me in a different direction. He was gently moving me away from what I thought was a dream come true. I don't know how to explain it, but I knew God was telling me, "No."

So I called the magician and told him, "Thank you for the amazing offer, but right now I can't do it." Trust me. Sometimes embracing God's mystery is not easy. But even at that time, I knew God's dream for me was better than my dream.

I knew God had a better perspective, that His ways were better than mine. So I trusted Him through the process of letting go of that dream. About six months later, I started volunteering in the youth ministry at my church. Over

the next ten years, I volunteered, interned, and upon graduating from seminary, I became the youth pastor. I loved doing youth ministry in the local church, but different people challenged me to step out and combine my ability to do illusions with my passion to preach. At that time, I was far more interested in continuing youth ministry. That is, until I read this one verse that shook me to my core. It changed everything. It was Romans 11:29, which says, "God's gifts and His call are irrevocable." It was the first time I saw calling and gifting intertwined and inseparable from one another. I knew I had to combine these two loves into one ministry.

About a month after reading that passage, I was at the local gym and in desperate need of something to distract me from the rigors of my workout. So I picked up a magazine that I don't normally read and started leafing haphazardly through the pages. Soon I saw the smiling picture of the magician I had met ten years earlier. Even though I hadn't seen him or even thought about that day for years, I recognized him right away.

As I read through the article, I found out that he was on trial for multiple counts of fraud. He had been a great magician and had used his skills to get bookings all over the world. However, he would invite college students to go on tour with him and then have them use their credit cards for his traveling expenses. He explained to them that he would take care of their credit card debt in the next city, but what really happened was that as soon as the students' credit cards had been maxed out, he would leave them stranded in some foreign city. He had literally abandoned these young adults all over the world!

I realized with one hundred percent certainty that this would have been me if I had gone with him. If I had not listened to God's voice guiding me, I would have been stranded, penniless, knowing no one, in a country where English probably wasn't spoken, and wondering how I would get home to my family.

Back at the gym, I realized just how much listening to God's voice mattered. For me, age 18 wasn't the right time to start doing magic full time. Becoming a magician at this point would have been far more about me and less about glorifying God. It would have been about me trying to fit into the world's plan for me and not waiting on God's plan for me. God had to shape me, teach me, and prepare me for a world-wide ministry. God had laid the foundation for me to start a new ministry of sharing God's life-changing message through captivating illusions.

THE CHICKEN STORY

Yeah, I know being an illusionist and pastor is an odd combination, and it wasn't an easy decision to make. I had been in youth ministry for almost 10 years when Jeff Harris, founder of Inroads Church, asked me, "Why haven't you combined sleight of hand and sharing God's Word into a ministry?"

I gave him my typical excuses: "I don't want to leave youth ministry" or, "Things are going great right now so why change?"

He laughed at my reasons and gave me his own: "I think you're just too chicken to do it." I called him a few choice names, we laughed, and then went on to talk about other stuff.

But like a catchy song, this conversation played again and again in my head. Over the next few weeks, I really thought about that statement. I had always been afraid to tell others that I did illusions. I didn't want them to associate the art of magic with some other (witch) craft. I loved to perform, but it was awkward saying, "Hey I'm a magician. Let me show you something."

As time went on, I thought I should at least seek God's heart on this. Was this something that He wanted me to do or was it just my own idea? After all, in my mind, there could be nothing better for me than combining my love of ministry with magic. I loved sharing God's Word with people and I also loved performing, practicing, and doing sleight of hand. So why not put these two passions together?

After spending much time in prayer, I began to seek counsel from the body of Christ. I went to my pastor, a random pastor in another town, an arbitrary counselor, my old youth pastor, and several others. Each of them said something along the lines of, "I don't know why you wouldn't leave youth ministry to begin this new ministry." This was both encouraging and terrifying. Thoughts raced through my head, like, "How will I support my family? What if I lose my house, car, etc.?" Yet God nudged me gently, reminding me that He was the Provider, He was the Sustainer, He was the Rock, and I needed to take refuge in Him.

After two years of wrestling with God in prayer and seeking guidance from the body of Christ, I had a conversation with Dan Monteverde, my old youth pastor. We hadn't seen each other in about six months and we both had very busy schedules. I wrote down all of my thoughts and questions so that I wouldn't be wasting any of his time.

We sat across the table from each other at a little sandwich shop in Sacramento, California. He said, "I know you have a lot on your mind because you have a list of questions a mile long!" Seeing my notebook full of questions, he suggested we start at the beginning and just work through my concerns until we were finished. I started by saying, "Dan, here is the thing: I know I must..." Dan abruptly interrupted me. "Danny," he said, "I don't care what else you have on those pages." A little surprised by his reaction, I swallowed slowly and knew a lesson was in store. "Whatever follows, you have to do it," he continued. "It is not a matter of if, but when. Anytime you make an 'I must' statement, you must do it. Period. It is only a matter of time. So whatever else follows, you must do it. But go ahead. I'll hear you out."

Needless to say, he was right. The answers were right there in front of me, but I didn't realize the very words "I must" became the answer to my prayers. Over the next few months, I would transition from being a youth pastor to a full-time performer/speaker. I would begin to pursue the God-sized dream of sharing God's transforming message through captivating illusions.

OLD MAN HANDS

When I have the privilege of speaking with teenagers, sometimes I will ask, "How many of you noticed my 'old man hands'?" Several hands will go up and I will see a few nods. I have old looking hands and they've looked about

100 years old since I was five. I am not joking. When I was a kid, other kids would make fun of my hands. I would see them snickering and pointing, "Look at that kid's old man hands!" The other characteristic about me that people made fun of was my voice. My speech cadence was slow and the "s" sound was slurred at times. Due to this I went to speech therapy until I was in fifth grade. So growing up, I was often made fun of for my hands and my voice.

Here is the crazy part: those are the two key aspects of my life that God is using to share His love with people around the world! The two things that others used to tear me down and say, "you don't fit in," have become instruments for His kingdom. The two things that were awkward, strange, and what I thought were my weaknesses, God has turned into strengths. The things that I perceived to be worthless, God is using for His glory. My hands and voice were never meant to fit in, they were always meant to stand out—that's the way God made me!

It doesn't matter how awkward, odd, or weird you might think you are. At times you might feel like you have two left feet, or maybe you were born without a limb, I don't know. What I do know is God

NEVER DOUBT WHO GOD DESIGNED YOU TO BE.

designed you for a purpose and has a plan to do amazing things with you. When we surrender our all to Him, He will do the impossible in and through us.

God uses the misfits, the quirky, the oddballs of this world to share His powerful message with the world. Never doubt who He has designed you to be. Forget the haters that are going to try to get you off course and instead get laser focused on God and He will direct your footsteps. His dream for you will always stretch you, and by his power, He will enable you to accomplish the things you know you "must" do.

ACTION PLAN

Take one weekend to stop all media. No texting, no social media, no movies, no video games, etc., and ask God to reveal His plans to you. This can be a very powerful way to hear God's voice.

During that weekend ask God:

What things are distracting me from being closer to you? What things are keeping me from hearing you?

What "must" you do? What are the things that you know God has designed you for? Complete this sentence: I know I must . . .

Consider these "I must" statements from the Bible:

1. "He must become greater; I must become less." John 3:30
2. "But he said, 'I must proclaim the good news of the Kingdom of God to the other towns also, because that is why I was sent.'" Luke 4:43

Take 10 minutes right now to be still. During this time, ask God to speak to you and reveal His purpose for your life.

GOD'S MIRACULOUS PROVISION

CHAPTER 6

GOD'S MIRACULOUS PROVISION

Following Jesus is dangerous. Think about it for a moment, you are following the One who can still tornados, can place planets into orbit and has the power to make hearts beat. It's a wonderfully frightful journey to follow Someone so powerful. Someone who has the ability to change the course of our lives with a simple word. Jesus has the power to provide for us the air we breathe or remove it instantaneously.

Sometimes we forget just how commanding and mighty Jesus is, especially if you are a teen who has grown up in the church, and we can easily become complacent:

Grace becomes ordinary.

Jesus' sacrifice becomes familiar.

God's love becomes normal.

The power of the Spirit becomes trivial.

Prayer becomes boring.

Life becomes mere existence.

But following Jesus is nothing less than extraordinary. God demonstrates his power in our lives in many ways, but one of those is through miraculous provision—God meeting our needs through supernatural circumstances or events outside of our control.

Sometimes God's miraculous provision puts us in awkward situations. I think this is God's way of saying, "Get over yourselves. Life isn't about you. It's about Me!" I think it puts a smile on His face when we follow Him through awkwardness to experience God deepening our faith.

We all feel awkward at times, but it's what we do with that awkwardness that helps shape and define us. There is a great story in the Bible (Matthew 17:24-27) about God providing in a miraculous way, but through an awkward situation.

Jesus and his unlikely group of misfits arrived in Capernaum, an ancient town in the Middle East. When they strolled into town, the temple-tax police, also known as bill collectors, or super enforcers, showed up and asked Peter if Jesus had paid His taxes for the temple. Peter told them, "Of course." Peter probably felt good, confident in his answer, until Jesus came in and put him in an awkward situation. Jesus asked Peter, "What do you think, Simon? From whom do the kings of the earth collect duty and taxes—from their own children or from others?" Peter gave the obvious answer, "From others." Jesus subtly told Peter that He did not need to pay the "temple tax" because this was His Father's house. He was the Son, so He was exempt, but Jesus told Peter, "so that we may not cause offense, go to the lake and throw out your line. Take the first fish you catch; open its mouth and you

68

will find a four-drachma coin. Take it and give it to them for my tax and yours."

There are two incredible truths I want to unpack from this story. First, this command from Jesus put Peter in a wonderfully awkward position. Peter was a fisherman by trade. He had caught thousands of fish and almost certainly never found one with a coin in its mouth. Imagine Jesus saying to you, "Go down to Taco Bell, buy Meal Deal #4, and inside the burrito there will be a $100 bill." It seems crazy. I imagine as Peter headed down to the water and some people walked by, the conversation might have gone something like this:

Random person 1: "Hey, Peter! What are you doing?"

Peter: "Um ... there is a fish out there with a coin in its mouth. Jesus wants me to catch it."

Other Guy 2: "You are fishing for money? Interesting (sarcastically). Did Jesus put money in thousands of fish? You know there are about a billion fish in there, right?"

Peter: "Yes. I know it sounds crazy."

Other Guy 3: "It is crazy, Peter. When are you going

JESUS IS ALWAYS SURPRISING US WITH HIS CONTROL OF THE ENTIRE UNIVERSE.

to stop following that crazy-wannabe teacher? How are you supposed to catch the only fish in the world with a coin in its mouth? Good luck with that! Let us know when you want to start hanging out again and stop following that weird guy. Fish don't have money in them, Peter, and money doesn't grow on trees! Come back to reality!"

What an odd request Jesus gave to Peter. He could have just made the coin appear behind Peter's ear, not sent him fishing for it. But Jesus is always surprising us with His control of the entire universe. Of all the fish in the world, Jesus was able to control Peter's line to catch the one fish with a coin in its mouth. Jesus was and is able to provide in miraculous ways.

One of my constant prayers is that God would provide in miraculous ways. To experience His miraculous provision, sometimes you have to take an awkward walk to the lake with your fishing line. Peter's faith and trust in Jesus was amazing. He didn't question Jesus' sanity. He just obeyed. In what areas do you need to just obey Jesus? God continues to provide in miraculous ways today.

The second truth I want to point out is this: God is at work upstream. What has to happen upstream for there to be a miracle downstream? What about the fish that had a coin in its mouth? How did it get there? I can picture some kid that shoved a coin in a fish's mouth. Imagine that his mom ran to him, saying, "What are you doing?! Let go of that fish! Stop shoving that coin into its mouth. We need that money!" Then imagine the kid smiled, saying, "God told me to do it." Years later, God had brought that fish right where it needed to be for Peter to catch it. That's working upstream!

Think about the power and confidence of Jesus telling Peter, "Take the first fish." Jesus didn't tell him to fish all day and all night until he caught the one with a coin in its mouth. Jesus was and is in control of everything in the universe including the billions of fish in that sea. Jesus did not hesitate, but had full confidence in telling Peter to grab the first fish.

But what about when God doesn't provide for us when we think He should? Jesus is still holding your life together—your junk, your struggles, your pain, your awkwardness, and your world that feels like it's falling apart. At any moment, He could call on ten thousand angels to come to your side to provide in miraculous ways. At any moment, He could bring comfort in the storm. At any moment, He could take away all of the pain. So why doesn't He?

Pain is God's way of bringing those who are far, close, and those who are close, closer. Pain brings the proud to their knees and the humble to prayer. Pain is God's reminder that we need Him every moment of every day. Pain reminds us that we are always desperate for a merciful God and pain reveals God's heart to provide for our eternal needs through that rugged cross. Pain is guaranteed but so is grace in the midst of suffering.

God is always providing for us. Sometimes, though, God's miraculous provision takes the form of enabling and equipping us to meet the challenges and pain of life that would otherwise defeat us. He doesn't necessarily rescue us from our problems, but He provides us comfort in our sorrow, patience in our trials, and the ability to overcome the sin that so easily entangles us. His spirit gives us the power to find joy in all circumstances and to love even when it feels impossible. No matter the situation, God provides us what we need to face the pain in our lives and even to show grace to those who have most wounded us.

PHIL: THE FINAL YEARS

After my biological father got out of prison, we lost touch again for another twelve years. I knew he had been released from prison, but I didn't know where he was living and I had no way of contacting him. Sometimes I would talk to one of his brothers, but nobody knew where Phil had gone. I continued doing the things that God called me to do and lived the life that I knew God had planned for me. One afternoon, my mom called and said she wanted to talk. She had that sound that all moms have when it's something serious.

My sister, brother, and I sat on the same couch, in the same living room where we had sat twelve years earlier, and

71

had a similar conversation. My mom went on to explain that Phil had experienced two heart attacks and the doctors had told him to get his affairs in order. The doctors gave him six months to live. My mom explained that she had his phone number and if we wanted to get in contact with him, it was up to us. My brother wanted nothing to do with him. My sister and I chose to meet with him.

We set up a meeting at Coco's restaurant in San Diego, California. It was there that I would meet the mysterious man that had haunted me, eluded me, and fascinated me. For the first time in my life I would sit right across the table from him, face to face, eye to eye, staring at a familiar yet completely unknown man. My heart raced. Thoughts flooded my mind. The few memories I had of him washed over me. I had thought about this moment a thousand times, but now that it was happening, I was rather speechless. The conversation was awkward, stilted, and kind of weird. What do you say to a man who abandoned you as a child? What kind of man does that? As some anger crept in, I reminded myself that God loved Phil just as he was and wanted to provide His mercy, His grace

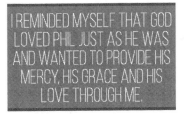

I REMINDED MYSELF THAT GOD LOVED PHIL JUST AS HE WAS AND WANTED TO PROVIDE HIS MERCY, HIS GRACE AND HIS LOVE THROUGH ME.

and His love through me. I reminded myself how much God had forgiven me and knew that I needed to completely forgive this man.

So we started talking about what he had been doing, about his health, and about our lives. I had a ton of questions and he did his best to answer them. Over the next six months, I met with Phil four times. I was trying to piece together broken stories, broken years, and broken lives. I was trying to answer questions that I had wanted to know for years, but there came a day when I decided I had to either forgive Phil and move on toward reconciliation or just let him go. Though forgiving the man who abandoned me as a child might have seemed like an impossible task at some point in my life, God had been working on my heart for many years, and as I grew in my faith of who God was and what he could accomplish in my life, I realized that God could give me the strength I needed to make amends with Phil. So I decided to reconcile. When I met with him that fourth time, I told him I would never ask a question about the past again. If he wanted to share something, that was great, but I was not going to press any further. To forgive him and to show him grace, I had to let him off the hook. I had to show him that God provides grace to broken people, even his broken life.

There were still questions that swirled through my head at times, but I decided it wasn't worth pursuing answers to the past. Instead, we moved forward into a new relationship. Reconciliation is never easy, especially with those who have hurt us the most, but sometimes reconciling is exactly what we need to do. Remember that Jesus calls us to forgive in all situations, but reconciliation is optional. In other words, we need to forgive because Jesus told us to forgive each other "just as in Christ God forgave you" (Ephesians 4:32). However, that doesn't necessarily mean we need to reconcile with a person that beat us, raped us, or harmed us in some other way.

The doctors gave him six months, but God gave him eight years. Over the next eight years of Phil's life, we met together for lunch, he came to some of my shows, and we would talk on a regular basis. Often times, Phil would mention the joy I brought to him. God enabled me to forgive Phil, and by being forgiven, he received a second chance at life. It gave him hope. He was so thankful for the grace God had given him through me.

Although I would never wish the suffering I

73

experienced from Phil's absence for 27 years of my life on anyone, I also know that God gave me miraculous provision in the form of grace towards my biological father, and has used my pain to bring healing and hope to others. God can use anything we surrender to Him, including our pain and suffering.

ACTION PLAN

Have you ever seen God provide for you in a miraculous way?

Make a list of blessings. In doing this, it will remind you of how God has been providing for you in amazing ways. See if you can get past 27 blessings.

How can you be God's hands and feet and provide for others through your talents and resources?

Who do you need to forgive? Ask God to help you to forgive that person. Maybe you need to do it face to face, maybe in a letter, but make a choice to forgive him/her.

Who do you need to reconcile with? In reconciling, you might just bring life to the lifeless.

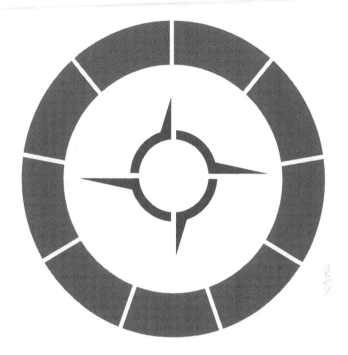

MAKE YOUR TEENAGE YEARS REMARKABLE

MARKED BY PROMISE

CHAPTER 7

MARKED BY PROMISE

Recently, I received a gift from my friend, Joe Castaneda. It was a book called The Compound Effect by Darren Hardy. It was a simple gift with a profound message: consistency creates powerful, life-transforming results. It's like the old story about a Chinese man who went to the Emperor and asked him for some rice. When the Emperor asked the man how much he desired, the man looked around and saw a chessboard. Pointing to one of the squares, he replied, "One grain of rice on this square, two on the next square, and four on the next." He continued, "Just double the number of grains on each square from the previous square." The Emperor didn't understand the power of doubling a grain of rice, not just once, but 64 times (the number of squares on the chessboard).

Do you realize how much rice the man asked for? He asked for 18,446,744,073,709,551,615 grains of rice. If you were to take the largest aircraft carrier in the world, the U.S.S. Nimitz, weighing about 100,000 tons, you would need to have one million Nimitz carriers on one side of a scale in order to balance out the amount of rice this Chinese man would have teeming on the other side of the scale. That's a lot of rice! And that's the power of the compound effect in our lives.

More importantly than gaining a boatload of rice, the compound effect illustrates how consistently trusting in God's promises radically changes the outcome of our lives. In 2 Peter, Peter writes, "[God] has given us his very great and precious promises, so that through them you may participate in the divine nature, having escaped the corruption in the world caused by evil desires." This verse is amazing! God has given us His "great and precious promises" so that we can "participate in the divine nature and escape the corruption in the world." When we live out His promises, we get to "participate in the divine nature." Getting to participate in the divine nature is like having 100,000 tons of rice to feed millions of people. It's like drinking out of a fire hose. It's like playing a video game in God-mode. We get to participate in what the infinite, immeasurable God is doing in and through us. Not only that, but by His promises we escape the corruption in the world that could tear us apart. Consistently participating in what God is doing and escaping what the world is doing creates a compound-like effect in our lives.

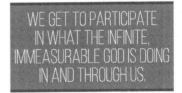

WE GET TO PARTICIPATE IN WHAT THE INFINITE, IMMEASURABLE GOD IS DOING IN AND THROUGH US.

When teens are consistent with forgiving, it creates incredible hope and inspiration for those around them.

When teens are consistent with giving grace, it changes families and it empowers people. Grace is contagious.

When teens are consistent with empowering others, a new generation of leaders rises up.

When teens are consistent in trusting in God's

promises, it is going to impact their lives and God's kingdom in a major way.

Joshua 21:45 reminds us that "not one of all the Lord's good promises to the house of Israel failed; every one was fulfilled." God's promises never fail. It's hard for us to wrap our minds around something that never fails. Our cars fail. Our appliances fail. Our relationships fail. Our leaders fail. Trust issues are inevitable because everything we know fails, but God doesn't fail. God's promises have never failed. To become the person God has designed us to be, we need to consistently trust in God's unfailing promises. Living out His promises unleashes the power of God in our lives.

ONE PROMISE CHANGES EVERYTHING

I want to unpack one promise in particular that has significantly changed my thinking over the years. This one promise has shaped me into a better man. That promise is found in Matthew 6 where Jesus tells us:

> "Your heavenly Father already knows all your needs, and He will give you all you need from day to day if you live for Him and make the Kingdom of God your primary concern."

Anytime there has been a crossroad in my life, this has been the promise I have gone to. Maybe you have wondered, "What should I do next? Should I take this class or that one? Should I go to this school or that one? Should I take this job or that one? Should I say yes or no?" Without question, this promise has marked my life and revealed exactly what I have needed to do.

The first truth I want to point out about this verse is that Jesus tells us that God is our "heavenly Father."

Sometimes it's hard to imagine God as your Father—your Dad. Maybe your dad missed what a treasure he had in you. Maybe your dad was the furthest thing from good and kind, but your heavenly Father is better than even the best earthly father.

He freely gives to you.

He delights in you.

He loves being with you.

He values you.

His love for you sent His Son to die a horrible death so you could have an abundant life. If your heavenly Father had a refrigerator, you would be all over it. Every day it would be covered with new pictures of you because He can't get enough of you. You are the apple of His eye.

Psalm 139 tells us that our Daddy thinks about us constantly. If we were to try to gather all of His thoughts about us, they would outnumber the sands on the seashore (Psalm 139:17). Our Father holds us in His arms (Deuteronomy 33:12). He is running toward us to embrace us. No matter how filthy we might feel, God can't wait to embrace us. He wants to throw a party and celebrate our coming to life (Luke 15).

Your heavenly Father cares for you more than you could ever imagine. Don't allow your past, your mess, or your thoughts about what a daddy is to hinder you from experiencing the fullness of Him as a Father. Let your God, your Dad, wipe away every tear from your eyes. Let Him embrace you. Let Him save you from your old ways and your old life. Let Him whisper into your ear, "You are my child. You are my sweet child. I love you! I have plans for you. Trust Me. Follow Me. I love you like no one else ever could."

Not only do we have a Dad who loves us, but Jesus reminds us that our heavenly Father "already knows all of [our] needs." Have you ever seen a child trying to hide something she broke from her parents? It's cute. She's covered in blue glitter with a guilty look on her face, hands behind her back trying to act like nothing happened. The parent takes one look and instantly knows what happened. In the same way, God already knows our thoughts before we ever express them verbally. So why should you want to tell Him about your life if He already knows? Because He's our Daddy. He wants to be in an intimate relationship with us. He wants us to come out of hiding and tell Him all of our struggles, fears, hopes, and dreams. He wants to hear from us and be close to us. We can tell Him everything because we know that in sharing our lives with Him, we can experience His grace, His wisdom, and His love. We can see His promises fulfilled in our lives and this will give us hope to sustain us day by day.

The second truth I want to highlight is that the promise of Matthew 6 contains two "and"s. I love this word. God is trying to get our attention. It's powerful. It would be more than enough for us to have God as our Father. But this powerful promise also says, "And He will give you . . ."

He gives freedom.

He gives hope.

He gives grace.

Isn't it fun to give gifts to a loved one? When you give someone the perfect gift and they smile from ear to ear, it's a wonderful feeling to know you made their day. God loves giving good gifts to His children. He loves surprising us with good things because He is a cheerful giver.

He is the giver of life.

He is the giver of joy.

He is the giver of love.

He is constantly looking for ways to give to His children, and ultimately, the Father gave us the greatest gift of all—His only Son. And Jesus, like His Father, was a giver and He gave us His life. In John 10:18, Jesus said, "No one takes my life from me. I give it up willingly!" That is the ultimate gift from the most amazing Giver. Jesus also wants to give us His Holy Spirit, which is His seal of approval on us. After Jesus sends the Spirit of God to live in us, the Spirit changes everything. From that point on, we no longer have God just with us, but we have God in us. God is literally transforming us from the inside out.

But wait, there's more! The rest of the verse goes on to say that our Father will give us "all [we] need from day to day." God promises to take care of us. I have heard, and experienced personally, countless stories of how God provided an exact amount of money for a bill at the perfect time (usually the 11th hour). God knows us intimately. He knows our every need physically, spiritually, relationally, emotionally, and financially. It's His desire, as our Dad, to provide for all of our needs.

HE KNOWS OUR EVERY NEED PHYSICALLY, SPIRITUALLY, RELATIONALLY, EMOTIONALLY, AND FINANCIALLY. IT'S HIS DESIRE, AS OUR DAD, TO PROVIDE FOR ALL OF OUR NEEDS.

Remember the widow from 1 Kings who went to

Elisha for help? Part of her story was the pain and loss of her husband. Even though God will be with us and provide for us through trials and troubles of this life, He does not remove us from such tragedies. He promises to meet our needs, not make our lives free from harm.

Remember how God provided for the wandering Israelites with manna from heaven?

Daily provided bread from heaven.

Daily cared for their needs.

Daily gave them enough for the present.

God does not say, "Here is a supply for the next year and we will talk after this supply runs out." No. God is involved in our lives from day to day. He wants to be there to wake you up in the morning, tuck you in at night, and be with you every moment in between. He is not a God who is far from us, but He is with us and in us.

I love that God constantly wants to provide for our needs. The Psalmist tells us to bring our requests before God and wait in expectation all day long (Psalm 5). We have a wonderful opportunity, every day, to meet with God and wait eagerly for Him to meet our daily needs. The joy comes not just in receiving, but joy comes in the privilege of having access to our God daily.

God promises to meet all our needs. However, there is one final aspect of this verse I want to highlight and that is the importance of the word "if." Jesus tell us our Father will meet all our needs "if [we] live for Him and make the Kingdom of God [our] primary concern."

"If" is a small yet powerful word. In Matthew 6, "if" is the key to unlocking God's promise to provide for all your needs from day to day. While God's love and salvation are free, some of His promises are conditional. It is the equivalent of a parent saying, "You can go to Disneyland if you get straight As." There's a requirement of the student. God requires certain things of us. In this promise, our needs being met hinges on two things. The first is if we "live for Him," and the second is if we "make the Kingdom of God our primary concern." If we want God to provide miraculously for us, if we want God to do amazing things in our lives, if we want to experience His blessings, and if we want to see Him fulfill His promises in our lives, then we must be willing to do the hard work of living for Him.

It's not that His expectation is perfection from us. No. We are all beautiful messes, but when we stumble, we should stumble forward. We should press on and humbly fall at His feet every single day, begging for forgiveness, grasping ahold of grace, and becoming empowered once again by the Spirit of God. Then we can move into a new day, full of God's power that is mightily at work within us. We must make a decision daily to live for our King.

You must choose to live for Him and make His kingdom your primary concern. I try to filter everything I do through those two standards: 1) Living for Him, and 2) making His kingdom my number one priority. Remember at the start of this section when I told you God's promise in Matthew 6 helps me with every decision I face? Well, here's how that works out in my life. If I have two big opportunities before me and I need to choose just one in the next 24 hours, I ask myself, "Which one of these options will give me the best opportunity to live for God more and to build His kingdom?" After doing this, it's usually apparent which opportunity I should take. If not, I continue to pray about it, seek wise counsel, and wait on God. If both opportunities give me the chance to live for God more and to build His kingdom, I just choose one! I pray for wisdom and I make a decision, trusting that God will direct my steps.

COMING OF AGE

For my son Brian's thirteenth birthday, I wanted to remind him that he was marked by the promises of God and show him tangible ways he could live for God and make the Kingdom of God his primary concern. We had a rite of passage ceremony celebrating the years of childhood and his transition into manhood. I wanted to carve out time with godly men who loved Brian and would speak the promises of God into his life.

On his birthday, Brian had no idea what was in store for him. He knew I was going to do something big, but he didn't know exactly what was planned. I bought him a new Bible and as the men arrived, I had them highlight their favorite verses. They also put notes next to those verses to encourage Brian to become the man God had designed him to be. After everyone arrived, Brian's youth pastor, Mike Thompson, and youth leader, Stephen Jarrett, blindfolded him and took him on a twenty minute off-roading adventure to an unknown location in the middle of the wilderness. Everyone else followed closely behind.

After being tossed back and forth in the truck, we brought him out of the vehicle, still blindfolded. We carefully walked him to the top of a six-foot high brick wall. I talked with Brian about the importance of trusting in God even when we can't see Him, reminding Brian that we live by faith and not by sight. At that moment, I had all the men hold out their hands, ready to catch Brian. I asked Brian to put his hands crisscross over his chest and then fall backwards into their arms. As you might imagine, he was very afraid. He was disoriented. If he was going to fall, he had to put his trust in me, his dad. After he successfully made the trust fall, I removed the blindfold and talked to him about the reality that he would go through trials in life that wouldn't make sense, but could trust in God, who would catch him every time.

At that point in my son's life, he was insecure about showing his bare chest. When we left the house, I made sure he was wearing his favorite shirt. It seemed like he would wear this shirt three or four times a week. He loved it that much. But this shirt represented childhood. I talked to him about how he had worn the shirt, had treasured the shirt, and how he needed to treasure childhood because he was now transitioning into manhood. Not that he was a man at that point, but he was no longer a boy and we weren't going to treat him like one anymore. At that point I asked him to rip off his shirt. He tore it off, exposing his bare chest. With the remains of the purple shirt in hand, he let out a barbaric yell. The men cheered loudly with him.

Brian's namesake, a man named Brian Wilmoth, then spoke to him about how Brian came into this world naked and naked he would eventually leave this world. But while he was here, he was to live for God and make the Kingdom of God his primary concern. He encouraged Brian to daily clothe himself with Christ. All of us laid hands on my son as Brian Wilmoth prayed over him. Then we put a new shirt on him, representing the new man he was becoming.

Brian has always enjoyed first-person shooter video games. Even though he has enjoyed these games, he had never shot a real gun before. This was his first time shooting a handgun, a rifle, and a shotgun, and we talked about the idea of being a protector. As a man, I explained, you protect your brother, you protect your sister, you protect your mom, and as a man you protect your family. You stand up for others. You look out for others. You stand up for the weak. You look out not only for your own interest, but for the interest of those around you as well (Philippians 2:4).

From there, we moved to the fire pit. I took out a watch and gave it to Brian (I'm honored to say that he's worn it every day since then). On the back of that watch is inscribed: "Brian, it's time to run your race." The inscription is a challenge for him to live every day with every moment for God and to make the Kingdom of God his primary concern.

I then took out two ancient coins, actual widow's mites, and gave them to him. I told him the story that Jesus told in the Gospels about the woman who gave everything she had. As I placed those widow's mites into Brian's hands, I reminded him that a man willingly gives everything he has. A man is not a hoarder. A man is not greedy. A man gives all he has to God.

Finally, it was time for the biggest gift. Each man in that circle either took out a letter and read it to Brian or spoke spontaneously. They spoke about the promises of God. They talked about the potential they saw in Brian. They poured into my son so he could truly live for God and become the man that God has designed him to be. They revealed the power of living for God and their experiences in making the Kingdom of God their primary concern.

This was a powerful moment for me and I believe it will stand as one of the most significant moments in life for my son Brian. I believe that day will serve as a reminder, throughout His entire life, of what it means to be a man marked by the promises of God.

ACTION PLAN

What promises do you need to lean on today? Write down 10 of God's promises. You can do a Google search for the top 10 promises of God.

For example:

"I can do all this through him who gives me strength." Philippians 4:13

"Have I not commanded you? Be strong and courageous. Do not be afraid; do not be discouraged, for the Lord your God will be with you wherever you go." Joshua 1:9

"The Lord will fight for you; you need only to be still." Exodus 14:14

Text a friend one of those promises or put one of them on your social media to encourage others.

It's hard to put God first in your life. What are some practical ways you can put Him first in your life?

MARKED BY FREEDON

CHAPTER 8

MARKED BY FREEDOM

Recently I returned home from a long trip and my wife was a little overwhelmed with the housework. The next day, while she was out, I decided I was going to clean. I started with the kitchen and made my way into the living room. I noticed that there was dust on some of the furniture. I was going to grab a cloth to wipe things down, but I wanted to do a superb job. That is when a wonderful idea came into my head—a leaf blower. Yes, that's what I needed. That would clean all the dust. Now, I don't know if you have ever turned on a 75-mph leaf blower in your house, but it's, well, amazing! I don't know why, but the first place I pointed my new weapon was under the stove. Not only did I blow dust out, but a Pokemon card and a swirl of other toys evacuated their shelter. Before I knew it, I was pointing this thing under the fridge, on top of the china cabinet and, let me just tell you, I would not have been surprised had a tumbleweed blown by. Huge clouds of dust engulfed me. The power! I "dusted" everything imaginable. Ten minutes later, I turned the blower off to survey my work. While I had successfully "dusted," it also looked like a hurricane had come through our house. The next hour was spent wiping and cleaning up the mess I had created.

The leaf blower brought everything out in the open. For us to be marked by freedom, we need God's Spirit to flow through our lives, bringing out those hidden sins and struggles that are weighing us down. I know it's hard because our lives might be scarred by divorce, abuse, neglect, loss, and death. Yet God is ready to blow away the spiritual dust and breathe new life into you. It's His life that frees you to live out the life He designed for you.

You are on a journey to be marked by your God. He wants to mark your life with freedom. One of my core beliefs is that God has a better plan for your life than you do. He has higher standards, bigger dreams, and a more abundant life for you than you could ever imagine. To experience the God-sized life that He has in store for you, you have to be free.

Free from your old life.

Free from old thinking.

Free from anything that is holding you back from creating a magnificent mark.

Do not think for a second that God does not have the resources to make your dream a reality. God has designed you for this moment, this space in time, for this day, for this life—do not waste it! This is your time in history to do something that will last for eternity. It is for such a time as this that He created you.

THIS IS YOUR TIME IN HISTORY TO DO SOMETHING THAT WILL LAST FOR ETERNITY.

You have one moment in time. One life. Your life. Live it for the

One who gives lavishly to all who ask. You only have today to make the most of every opportunity. Today is the day that the LORD has made, let us be glad that we have this moment, this life, and this dream. Seize this moment! Seize this day! It's the only one you have. Live free because it's the way God designed you.

Jesus told us that "If the Son sets you free, you are free indeed." The Son, Jesus, has set you free (John 8:36). You need to live out that freedom. Sometimes you feel chained when there are no chains, drowning when you are above the water, and trapped when you are really free. Even though we are free in Christ there are certain struggles and sins that hold us back from experiencing the freedom God desires us to have. I want to give you tools to help you overcome anything that might be holding you back so that you can experience freedom today.

CHANGE YOUR FOCUS

Our focus changes the course of our life. What we focus on consumes our time, our thoughts, and determines our future. Stop focusing on your problems and start focusing on solutions. When you are at church, what are you focusing on? When you eat lunch with your family, what are you focusing on? When you watch the game, what's your focus? Don't let the ring of your phone determine your focus.
Recently, my boys and I were setting up the "man cave." This is where we turn an ordinary garage into an Xbox playin', soda drinkin', bean bag loungin', big screen watchin' "man cave." As they were setting up the projector, they noticed the movie they were trying to play was out of focus. This really bothered them. They kept saying, "Dad, fix it," but I didn't. I let it stay out of focus while I continued to set everything up. Eventually, they figured out how to focus the screen, but it's

amazing how, when things are a little out of focus, we seem unable to move on.

God wants to give you crystal-clear messages. He wants you to have a life that is focused. You need to dial into Him every day so that the fuzzy world around you becomes clear. The clarity of His message is given throughout the Bible. 2 Corinthians 4:18 tells us that "we fix our eyes not on what is seen, but on what is unseen. For what is seen is temporary, but what is unseen is eternal." Maybe today you say, "I am no longer going to focus on how bad things are or how out of focus my life seems. Today I am going to draw a line in the sand and be focused on God and His goodness." Focusing on His message reminds us that we are free. It shapes us and moves us toward the God-sized life He intends for us. His message is wrapped in the words and life of Jesus. Focus on Jesus every day and you will experience freedom.

1. CONFESSING TO ONE ANOTHER

A lot of us have a secret sin or struggle that we return to over and over again. Maybe it's gossip. Maybe it's pornography. Maybe it's wearing different masks (acting one way online, another at church and as someone completely different at home). Something that we are ashamed to admit to others but we freely confess to God. We tell God we will never do it again but we do. So we create a cycle of confessing to God but not finding the strength to stop it. We go to God and tell him how sorry we are but then we go out and do the exact same thing. And the cycle repeats.

We need to be honest with God and with ourselves and confess our sins to Him. But the Bible tells us that we also need to "confess [our] sins to each other and pray for each other so that we may be healed" (James 5:16). If you have confessed to God over and over again, but you have not changed your ways, you need to confess to another believer.

You need to come out of hiding. Confession with our brothers and sisters is a must. It's not that confession to God isn't important – it absolutely is. But another fallen, broken, messy teenager, youth leader, or someone who loves Christ can remind you of God's love, compassion, and forgiveness. God created us. He knows how stupid we can be sometimes, but there is healing that can happen when we share our struggles and sins with other believers. Confessing leads to the healing and freedom that God desires for us.

2. BOUNDARIES

Set up boundaries. It's extremely important to set limits for yourself, and one way to ensure this is to get someone to keep you accountable—someone you can share the struggles you have with and who can help you stay on the right path. For example, I travel a lot so I have another guy who travels on the road with me to keep me accountable. We have set up a "no TV" policy. It's not like it is the law, but it is just a consistent boundary. This keeps us from doing meaningless things on the road, and assures that we avoid watching anything questionable or inappropriate. Boundaries are like guardrails. They keep you from regrets. Boundaries aren't meant to hinder your life, but rather they free you from the traps that so easily entangle us and remind us to "run with perseverance the race marked out for us" (Hebrews 12:1).

3. TRIGGERS

A trigger can be defined as anything that heightens your temptation. It could be a place, or a person, or a certain TV show. For example, a person who struggles with her self-image might spiral downward after looking at magazines of women who appear perfect. Or the guy who is striving to control his anger might be left feeling enraged every time he gets a phone call from his dad. Get to know your triggers.

Is it when you are alone? Is it when you are stressed? Is it when you are bored? Is it when you stay up late? Is it when you watch R-rated movies? Is it when you are online? Is it when you go to a certain friend's house? Is it when you listen to certain music? You have to take a good look at your life and be honest with yourself about the things that trigger your struggles. Let your accountability partner know your triggers.

Sharing your triggers will help your accountability partner pray for you so that you can experience freedom. It will also remind you that keeping little secrets hinders your ability to grow closer to God. It is always difficult sharing the real struggles going on in your life but the more you do, the less hold the struggle has on you.

4. JAR YOUR SYSTEM

Usually, the best solution we have when we are tempted is to pray or read the Bible. But other times, we may need to jar our systems. What I mean by this is that when we are tempted, sometimes we literally can't focus on any other thought and find it extremely difficult to pray or read God's word. So, jar your system by going for a walk, riding your bike, drawing a picture, watching a funny movie, listening to loud music, boxing with your sister, playing the drums, or just doing something you love to do. By doing this, we can sometimes reboot our minds so that when we return to reading or praying, we have fresh perspective and are able to retackle the problem or temptation.

In doing something we enjoy, it jars our system just enough to remind us that God is greater than our pain, our trials, our past, and our feelings.

5. DEVELOP AN ACTION PLAN

Develop an action plan. This is your line in the sand to experience freedom. For example, let's say your parents are leaving for the weekend, and you know that all of your temptations increase when they are away. Their leaving triggers ideas of partying, or going to a friend's house you are not supposed to, or going on websites you don't need to be on. I am sure you can think of other dumb things teenagers might do when their parents are away.

You need a plan of action to be successful while your parents are gone. Here is a sample plan of action:

- Wake up early so you will be ready to face the day with God's grace and strength. Spend time with God in the morning asking Him for help and direction.
- Memorize Scripture. Take a verse or a passage and write it on a note card. Keep it on you throughout the day. Then take time to pray and meditate on that verse every chance you can get.
- Call your accountability partner before your parents leave. Let him or her know your plan.
- If your parents are believers you might even tell them your plan.

This is just an idea of what an action plan might look like. The point is that an action plan changes the course of your outcome.

Changing your focus, confessing to one another, setting up boundaries, knowing your triggers, jarring your system, and having an action plan give you the ability to break the cycle of giving into temptation. God longs for you to experience freedom but we have to choose freedom. Jesus has set us free from sin and we no longer have to live in bondage, but it's not enough to know what to do, you have to make a choice to do it. Living free will bring you the peace you long for and open up your eyes to the incredible plan God has for you.

ACTION PLAN

What sins do you need to confess to someone?

Make a decision right now to confess to someone you trust by the end of the day. Ask them to pray for you.

What are your triggers for this sin and what can you do to avoid them?

What things can you do to jar your system when you feel temptation taking over? Write down several ideas.

Write down, "As of today, by God's grace, I will no longer (fill in the blank)."

Write down, "As of today, by God's grace, I will (fill in the blank)."

MARKED BY WISDON

CHAPTER 9

MARKED BY WISDOM

NUMBER YOUR DAYS

The day my father died is etched in my mind forever. I was home from a trip for less than 24 hours. I was on my way to the movies with my family when my wife and I got into a squabble over getting candy at a CVS market or getting it at the movie theater. I told her that the movie would sell out quickly so it would be best if we just got it at the theater. She was convinced that we had time so we went to the CVS and got the candy. When we arrived at the theater, the tickets were sold out.

As we were driving home, I got a call from my sister: "Call the hospital," she said. "Phil isn't doing well." I called and heard the news that brought tears to my eyes: "Your father has passed." The next moments, between praying, dropping kids off at the house, and driving down to the hospital, are still a blur.

I entered the hospital to lots of hugs from family

103

members. The nurse explained that they had done everything they could and that she was sorry for our loss. I entered his room and held his cold hand for the last time. The family gathered and I prayed a tearful, broken prayer.

Late that night, my wife and I drove back to our home. Three hours later, I would be on a plane to my next event. Had my wife not insisted on getting candy from the CVS, I would have gotten my way, turned off my phone in the movie, and missed my opportunity to say, "Goodbye."

Since then, there have been numerous times I have woken up in a sweat. Nightmares. You see, I honestly don't know whether Phil is in heaven or hell. The very thought haunts me. It breaks me. It compels me to share God's love, God's grace, and God's purpose with everyone I meet.

Where is your life going?

Like Phil, all of us will die and on our tombstone will be our name, the date we were born, and the date we died. Between those two dates will be a dash. That dash represents your life. What will your dash be about? Will it be about your story or His story?

You have an incredible opportunity to make your teenage years count.

Make your dash count!

Ask God to teach you to number your days, to make the most of every opportunity, and to make your moments matter. As a teenager, you are in a unique position to impact the world, but you

YOU HAVE AN INCREDIBLE OPPORTUNITY TO MAKE YOUR TEENAGE YEARS COUNT.

desperately need God's wisdom to guide you. God's wisdom is what will help you make the right choices, and ensure that when you get to the end of your days, you will have lived remarkably.

So how do we get this wisdom? A great place to start is with Solomon, who, the Bible tells us, had wisdom "greater than the wisdom of all the people" he lived around (1 Kings 4:30). Solomon received such divine wisdom because he was willing to be in the right place, offer sacrifice to the Lord, and ask for wisdom from God.

POSITIONED TO RECEIVE WISDOM

"Solomon loved the Lord . . . The most important [place] of worship was at Gibeon, so the king went there and sacrificed 1,000 burnt offerings. That night the Lord appeared to Solomon in a dream, and God said, "What do you want? Ask, and I will give it to you!" (1 Kings 3:3-5)

1 Kings tells us that "Solomon loved the Lord" and because of his love, he went to "the most important" place of worship – Gibeon. Solomon's love was the starting point for his actions. Solomon could have sacrificed anywhere, but out of love for God, he chose to give his best and go to the most important place, and his being in the right place was his first step towards wisdom.

Solomon may have learned the lesson of being in the right place from his father, David, who made the mistake of being in the wrong place. King David (remember the guy who took down Goliath?) and the beginning of his fall that led to adultery, murder, the loss of his son, and heartbreak began with David not being where he was supposed to be.

2 Samuel 11:1 says, "In the spring, at the time when kings go off to war, David sent Joab out with the king's men and the whole Israelite army. They destroyed the Ammonites and besieged Rabbah. But David remained in Jerusalem."

Where was David supposed to be? The kings, including David, were supposed to be at war, but David stayed behind.

It doesn't seem like that big of a deal. I mean, after all, what was the problem with staying home one day and relaxing? The problem is that David was not where he was supposed to be. Because he "remained," he missed God's plan for his life on that day. The passive action of remaining led to a world of disaster for David. While he was home and not at war, he ended up having an affair with Bathsheba, conceiving a child, and then having her husband murdered to try to cover his own sin. Had he sought God for wisdom, he would have been saved from a world of shame and loss that became inevitable.

I wonder how many of your problems could be solved if you had the wisdom to stay when God says "stay," and to go when God says "go"? Are you where you are supposed to be right now? If not, close this book, get on your knees, beg God for mercy, and get to where you are supposed to be. The sin of not doing something is just as dangerous as the sins we commit.

Unlike his father, Solomon positioned himself in the best place where he could worship God. This is the pattern of a man after God's heart. Although worship is constant and we are designed to worship day and night in wild abandonment to our God, when we carve out a special time to be with God, it should be the most important place for us. It should be a place that will get us away from the distractions of the world so that we can focus all of our being on the One we worship. Jesus, Himself, got up early in the morning while it was still dark and went to a "certain place" to meet with His Father (Mark 1:35). What place makes you feel like heaven is tilted toward you? What place opens up your heart to worship? One of the questions I ask myself almost every day is, "Where can I go and meet with God?" (Psalm 42:2)

SACRIFICE LEADS TO WISDOM

Solomon positioned himself for the Lord's appearing by going to the most important place and then giving his best. The Bible tells us that Solomon sacrificed "1,000 burnt offerings." We live in a day and age when sacrificing animals is a foreign concept. Even talking about putting your puppy on the altar is horrifying. Yet, that's what was going on. They gave their best and most loved animals to God as a sacrifice.

In the Old Testament, some offerings were required and others were voluntary acts of worship. The burnt offering was voluntary. This was important because it showed the hearts of those giving their offering freely. In short, a burnt offering was giving the best bull, lamb, or bird to be sacrificed to the LORD. The animal to be given was slaughtered and the priest sprinkled the blood on the altar. I know this seems gross, but there is a point. The animal was then skinned and cut into pieces. The priest burned the pieces throughout the night. Then the priest changed his clothes and brought the ashes from the burnt offering outside the Israelites' camp.

A burnt offering showed one's devotion to God as an act of worship.

Solomon's sacrifice of 1,000 burnt offerings was so over the top that it should astonish us. One bull sacrificed, then another, then another, again and again. Fifty-seven skins, up to 248, then 733, almost there at 891, and then finally 1,000 sacrificed! Each animal was slaughtered and cut into pieces as an act of worship – an act of love to and for his Lord. How many days did this take? As each bull was slaughtered it was as if Solomon was shouting, "I love You! I love You! I love You! You can have my best! You can have everything! It's all Yours! I love You!"

107

ASK GOD FOR WISDOM

It's important to note that it's only after Solomon has positioned himself in the right place and offered his sacrifices to the Lord that God appears to Solomon in a dream and says "What do you want? Ask and I will give it to you!" Solomon was the wisest man to ever walk the face of the earth, but what led to his wisdom? He asked for it. Solomon could have asked for anything, but he said, "Give me wisdom and knowledge, that I may lead this people" (2 Chronicles 1:10). Had he asked for wealth, God would have given it to him, but because he humbly asked for wisdom, God gave him wisdom and wealth and honor. God loves to give generously to His people, especially people that position themselves humbly at His feet as Solomon did.

This concept of asking God seems like such a simple thing, but it's one that the Bible teaches us over and over again. Jesus said, "Ask and it will be given to you; seek and you will find; knock and the door will be opened to you" (Matthew 7:7). James reminds us that "if any of you lacks wisdom," — that's all of us—"ask our generous God, and he will give it to you" (James 1:5). God is the giver of wisdom and He gives freely to all who ask Him for it. We need to ask and wait patiently as God gives us wisdom from beyond this world.

Your teenage years may be full of trials, troubles, and heartache, and sometimes complicated choices. Do you tell the truth and get grounded or tell a small lie so you

> GOD IS THE GIVER OF WISDOM AND HE GIVES FREELY TO ALL WHO ASK HIM FOR IT. WE NEED TO ASK AND WAIT PATIENTLY AS GOD GIVES US WISDOM FROM BEYOND THIS WORLD.

can be with your friends this weekend? Do you tell your best friend "no" because you know it's wrong or do you remain silent? How do you know what college you should go to? God's wisdom will change the course of your life if you, like Solomon, are willing to follow God, give him your best, and ask Him for the discernment we all desperately need.

ACTION PLAN

How can you make your dash count? How are you going to leave a magnificent mark?

Take time to write out a prayer to God. Ask Him for wisdom for specific things in your life.

What are some ways that you can tell God you love Him today?

Make a plan to get up early to meet with your God. Put it on your calendar and do it!

LEAVING A MAGNIFICENT MARK

EPILOGUE

LEAVING A MAGNIFICENT MARK

YOUR SIGNATURE IS YOUR MARK

What does your signature say about you? What would you like it to say? My good friend Steve is an airplane mechanic for UPS. His attention to detail is absolutely remarkable and his knowledge of how an aircraft works is exceptional. It's a good thing, too. You see, when Steve signs the repair log stating that he fixed a broken part or installed a new component on a plane, he is legally and ethically responsible for all of the lives on that aircraft. His signature means that he is vouching for the working condition of that plane. Steve's work is marked with excellence, knowledge, integrity, and passion.

Do you remember working on signing your name? I remember ignoring several teachers in junior high school as I developed the perfect signature. My binders had pages full of my various attempts and styles. Even then I knew my signature was important and I wanted it to look just right.

What if we carved out time, not just to work on what our signatures look like, but to work on what our signatures mean? When someone sees your name, what does it stand for? Would any of the following ideas be connected to your name?

- God's love
- God's grace
- God's excellence
- Passion
- Purpose
- Creativity
- Promise
- Freedom
- Wisdom

Your signature is your mark. Your signature carries some serious weight—it reflects who you are, what you believe, and the mark you are making in this world. What is your signature? How do you want people to remember you?

MAGNIFICENT MARK

I don't want to go through the motions of life and settle for average. I want to plant seeds of awesomeness that will impact the world. I want to live with significance. My deepest desire is to do something that matters and, ultimately, I want to leave a magnificent mark.

Leaving a mark isn't about becoming famous, rich, or powerful. It's about doing the maximum with what God has given you. If you are going to leave a magnificent mark, you have to decide what mark you want to leave as an expression of your life and then go after that in small ways every day.

What are you doing with your life that matters? What mark are you leaving?

Your life matters.

Your story counts.

You only have one life to live. Live it intentionally. Dream God-sized dreams. Leave a magnificent mark and inspire others to leave theirs!

ABOUT THE AUTHOR

Danny Ray is first and foremost an incredible husband and father of three children. In addition to authoring this book, he is a pastor with his Master's of Divinity who travels the world sharing God's Word. But what makes Danny a unique speaker is his God-given talent for doing incredible magic tricks and illusions. He uses these illusions to captivate audiences and make the messages memorable for a lifetime. He has partnered with over 1,400 ministries and performed for and spoken to over a million people. His illusions and messages have taken him to all 50 states and to 17 countries. And on a smaller scale, Danny has worked with the youth group at his church in order to stay current with teens and what they are going through.

Danny and his family live in sunny California where he continues to strive to live a ReMarkable life.

To have Danny at your next event go to:
www.nowaydannyray.com

 @nowaydannyray

 @nowaydannyray

 @nowaydannyray